Securing Your Future

A Practical Guide To Navigating Social Security Disability Benefits For Claimants And Their Families

Lisa R. Lang, Esq.

Jacobs & Whitehall

9600 Escarpment Blvd
Suite 745-282
Austin, TX 78749
(888) 570-7338
www.jacobsandwhitehall.com

Ordering Information:

Quantity sales. Special discounts are available on quantity purchases by corporations, associations, and others. For details, contact the publisher at the address above.

Orders by U.S. trade bookstores and wholesalers. Please contact Jacobs & Whitehall: Tel: (888) 570-7338 or visit www.jacobsandwhitehall.com.

Printed in the United States of America

Published in 2024

ISBN: 978-1-963063-18-9

DEDICATION

This book is dedicated to my Mom:

She taught me that despite any limitations, her love and generosity know no bounds.

She shows that giving from the heart is one of the most powerful acts.

Testimonials

"I am so impressed with my attorney, Lisa. Out of all that paperwork, she pulled out information on my neck injury from 2009 and presented it to the Judge. This evidence made all the difference. Lisa gets a 10 in my book, and everyone at Empowered Disability was great."

– Greg

****

"I am extremely happy with Empowered Disability's service. I was trying to get disability for 20 years and I was so happy when I won."

– Sherry

****

"Lisa Lang was great. I had lots of questions at first, and you answered my questions. Everything went smoothly and I got a win. Your service was great."

– Kimberly

****

DISCLAIMER

This publication is intended to be used for educational purposes only. No legal advice is being given, and no attorney-client relationship is intended to be created by reading this material. The author assumes no liability for any errors or omissions or for how this book or its contents are used or interpreted, or for any consequences resulting directly or indirectly from the use of this book. For legal or any other advice, please consult an experienced attorney or the appropriate expert, who is aware of the specific facts of your case and is knowledgeable in the law in your jurisdiction.

Lisa Lang Law, LLC.
dba Empowered Disability
5200 SW Meadows Rd, Ste 150
Lake Oswego, OR 97035
www.lisalanglaw.com
(888) 638-SSDI (7734)

TABLE OF CONTENTS

"We treat our clients like family – as family members of people with disabilities, we're here to stand with you and your loved ones, offering the understanding and support only family can give."

INTRODUCTION

My Background And Experience

I've been an attorney since 2001, and over the years, I've developed a deep focus on Social Security law. Since 2011, I have exclusively handled Social Security cases, working with both Supplemental Security Income (SSI) and Social Security Disability Insurance (SSDI). I am licensed in both Washington and Oregon, as well as in federal courts, including the Ninth Circuit Court of Appeals - and because Social

Security law operates at the federal level, the information I share in this book will be relevant to adults throughout the United States.

Why Social Security law? My interest in this field is heavily rooted in my childhood. My mother lives with multiple sclerosis. Her struggles, battles, and strengths deeply shaped me as a person and planted an early desire to help people like her and families like my own. Because of this, I knew early on that my purpose in life was to be of service to the underrepresented in society, providing them with assistance that they would not be able to find elsewhere.

When I first began my legal career, I joined a nonprofit legal services office in Oregon. There, I had the privilege of working directly under an attorney who was handicapped. Our work together only deepened my understanding of the challenges faced by individuals with disabilities, both in their personal lives and in the workplace. It's this understanding and commitment to supporting others that I've brought with me through every stage of my professional growth.

Eventually, I knew that I was destined to only practice SSDI/SSI law, and sought out a mentor – a decision that became pivotal to my career. In 2011, after six months of working together, I purchased my mentor's practice and have continued to hone my legal skills as an exclusive Social Security Disability attorney ever since.

Over the years, I've built relationships with national law firms and organizations like the National Organization of Social Security Representatives, connections that have allowed me to advocate for clients across the United States and for changes in the law that can benefit anyone living with a disability.

Ultimately, my mission is to guide people through this process with compassion and expertise, and this book is one more way I hope to fulfill that mission. The more prepared you are for the road ahead, the better your chances of finding the outcome you need. It is my hope that these pages will provide you with the resources and empowerment you need to navigate complex SSI and SSDI laws with clarity and confidence.

Who This Book Is For

Though I've helped thousands of people over the years, there is one case in particular that has always stood out for me.

A veteran with post-traumatic stress disorder had been referred to me by the Oregon State Bar and was experiencing severe emotional trouble. I took him in and walked him through the process. He was struggling so much with his condition that he was too frightened to leave his home – so I personally went to pick him up to make sure that he could get to his hearing. When we arrived, we went in front of a judge known to be tough and unyielding… *and won the case on the spot.*

I see this particular man in every client I've helped since, and I would like this book to empower you to fight and win as he did. If you're seeking SSI and SSDI benefits, you are likely vulnerable, unsure of the resources available, and truly struggling in life. You need thoughtful answers in plain English, and you need to be prepared for the road ahead.

Unfortunately, many clients assume that the Social Security application and claims process is passive. In other words, many clients assume their lawyer will do all the work. The truth is, both disability claimants and their attorneys are up against a massive government agency during the claims process. Even with an excellent lawyer by your side, it is also up to you to take an active role in the process, building your case so that you can get the benefits that you need.

Because of this, I'm deeply committed to educating people about this process and providing the support they need. So, while many other books about Social Security law are written for lawyers, this book was written to educate and empower the people and families who are going through the process of filing an SSI or SSDI claim - and likely facing one of the most difficult times in their lives.

If your goal is to give yourself the best chance at having your claim approved, you need a step-by-step resource that clearly outlines what you will need to know along the way and how to act in your best interest throughout the process - but you can't impactfully be proactive if you don't know what to do or how to do it. The key to a successful case is **consistency and persistence**. My sincere hope is that this book will be that guide.

CHAPTER ONE:

SOCIAL SECURITY DISABILITY CLAIMS 101

What Is Social Security Disability?

Social Security benefits for disabled individuals come in different forms. The primary types are Social Security Disability Insurance (SSDI), which most people think of when referring to Social Security disability, and Supplemental Security Income (SSI), which also provides benefits for disabled individuals, but that are low income. There are smaller subsets of benefits as well, such as disabled adult child benefits, child supplemental security benefits, and Disability for Blindness, but those fall outside the focus of this book.

My practice focuses primarily on SSDI and SSI, programs that provide monthly income to people with disabilities who are no longer able to work. Of course, these terms are similar-sounding and easily confused with one another, so let's break down who these benefits are for and how they differ.

The Difference Between Social Security Disability Insurance Vs. Supplemental Security Income

Both SSDI and SSI offer monthly income for disabled people who can no longer work, but differ in who they benefit, and what they are designed to do.

Social Security Disability Insurance (SSDI)

Called **Title II** by the Social Security Administration, SSDI is a long-term disability benefit for people who are no longer able to work due to serious illness or injury.

This program provides a financial bridge to retirement by offering monthly income to individuals who become disabled before they reach retirement age. This prevents the need for early retirement withdrawals, allowing for a more financially stable future. Once the person reaches full retirement age, SSDI benefits convert to regular retirement benefits.

To understand how SSDI works, it's helpful to remember that your Social Security contributions act like an insurance policy for the future. SSDI is funded through payroll taxes, so the amount you receive depends on how much you've paid into the system during your working years. As a result, the more you've earned and contributed, the higher your SSDI benefit will be.

If you stop working, your contributions stop as well, and eventually, your SSDI eligibility may expire. This expiration is known as your "date last insured," and if you cannot prove you were disabled before that date, you may no longer be eligible for SSDI, unless you return to work and contribute back into the system.

Supplemental Security Income (SSI)

Also known as **Title XVI**, this program is for disabled people who have limited financial means and do not have enough work credits to qualify for SSDI. It also helps people who have been out of work for so long that their SSDI benefits have expired.

Unlike SSDI, which is based on past earnings, SSI provides a fixed amount. In 2025, the maximum SSI payment for an individual will be $967 per month. This amount increases each year with cost of living adjustments. While this may seem modest, it serves as critical financial support for those in need. For more information, visit www.ssa.gov/cola.

Medicare & Medicaid

It's important to keep in mind that if you qualify for SSDI, you may also qualify for Medicare. Normally, Medicare isn't available until retirement age, but under SSDI, you can receive Medicare earlier.

For those who qualify for SSI, Medicaid becomes available instead. Both programs are vital for individuals who lose their jobs or can no longer work due to a disability, as they provide access to healthcare that may otherwise be unaffordable.

Determining Which Benefits To Apply For

When deciding which benefits to apply for, it's essential to evaluate your work history and financial situation. If you have a substantial work history and have accumulated enough work credits, applying for SSDI may be your best option, as it's generally more stable and secure. You can check your eligibility by signing up for a *My Social Security* account at the SSA's website, **www.ssa.gov/myaccount**, which will indicate whether you have enough credits for SSDI and provide updates on your claim status.

To qualify for SSDI, you typically need 40 work credits, with 20 of them earned in the last 10 years before your disability onset. Each credit represents a quarter of coverage based on earnings, so if you've worked steadily over the years, you'll likely meet this requirement. There are lesser work credits needed if your disability began before age 31.

If you don't have enough work credits, you may qualify for SSI if your income and assets are limited.[1] Generally, those eligible for SSI are individuals with limited work history and financial resources, and who are not financially supported by a spouse.

It's worth noting that, while you won't receive both SSDI and SSI at the same time, applying for both can still be beneficial. For example, if your SSDI payment is below the basic SSI amount (currently $967 per month in 2025), SSI may provide additional funds to meet this minimum. Additionally, if your SSDI eligibility has expired but you meet the requirements for SSI, you may still qualify for SSI benefits.

In summary, if you qualify for SSDI, that's generally the best option. However, if you're uncertain about eligibility or are facing financial hardship, applying for both SSDI and SSI may maximize your potential benefits.

---

[1] Claimants who became disabled prior to age 31 need fewer quarters of coverage.

Other Types Of Disability Insurance

There are other less common types of disability insurance that may be helpful to you and your family if you meet certain criteria or fall into certain categories.

Disabled Adult Child

A *disabled adult child* is someone over the age of 18 but under 22 who has been found disabled. These individuals are considered "disabled adult children" because they have never been able to work (substantial gainful activity) and will not be able to work SGA, yet they are still classified as dependents under the Social Security system. [2]

In many cases, this situation arises when a child has been receiving SSI benefits while younger, but loses eligibility upon turning 18 due to the stricter adult disability standard. If they meet this adult standard and their parent is receiving Social Security benefits or SSDI, the child can collect a portion of their parent's benefits.

---

[2] 42 U.S.C. § 402(d)(1); 20 C.F.R §§ 404.350-404.368.

In some cases, individuals may apply for disabled adult child benefits long after turning 22, as long as they can prove they were disabled before that age. This often happens when a parent retires, and the family needs to ensure their child will continue to get the financial support they need.

Child Supplemental Security

If a family is low income and the child meets the medical requirements for disability—such as being unable to function at the same level as other children their age—the parents can collect SSI on behalf of the child until the child turns 18. The child must meet specific criteria for disability, but essentially, the standard revolves around significant impairments that prevent them from functioning as their peers do. [3]

Blindness

The Social Security Administration defines blindness as being unable to correct vision in your best eye to 20/200, even with corrective lenses. You may

[3] 42 U.S.C. § 1382c(a)(3)(C)(i), 20 C.F.R. §416.906.

also be described as blind if your field of vision is 20 degrees or less, even with glasses or contact lenses. [4]

Both SSDI and SSI programs provide monthly income for individuals with blindness and are managed by the Social Security Administration, with similar coverage requirements in terms of work credits. If you meet these qualifications, you may qualify for monthly income.

The eligibility standard here is the same as it is for other disabilities. However, those who are blind have a longer "date last insured" period, giving them more time to prove their disability after they stop working. As a result, I approach these cases just like other SSDI claims, with the added consideration of the extended period for proving disability.

Medical Eligibility: Defining "Disability" Under SSI & SSDI

The medical requirements to prove your disability are the same under SSI and SSDI. To be frank,

---

[4] 42 U.S.C. §§ 416(i)(l); 1382c(a)(2); 20 C.F.R. §§ 404.1581-404.1587 and 416.981-416.987.

the Social Security Administration (SSA) does not give you the benefit of the doubt when you apply and will look at your case and assume that you are not disabled. It is up to you, rather, to prove to them that you are disabled and unable to work substantial gainful activity. But what *exactly* will you need to prove to the SSA?

Impairment

Firstly, you must demonstrate the existence of an "impairment"—an anatomical, physiological, or psychological abnormality that can be verified through medically "acceptable clinical and laboratory diagnostic techniques."[5] Furthermore, your documentation of the existence of your impairment must come from medical professionals defined by SSA's regulation as "acceptable medical sources." Once the existence of an impairment is established, all of the medical and non-medical evidence is considered in assessing impairment severity.

Some "Acceptable medical sources" include, but not limited to, Licensed physicians (M.D. or D.O)

---

[5] 42 U.S.C. § 423(d).

Licensed psychiatrists or licensed or certified psychologists, (Psy.D, Ph.D); Licensed optometrists (O.D) Licensed podiatrists (DPM) for impairments of the foot, or foot and ankle only. Qualified speech-language pathologists for speech or language impairments only (SLP); Licensed audiologists (AUD); Licensed advanced practice registered nurses (APRN or APN); advanced registered nurse practitioners (ARNP) for impairments within his or her licensed scope of practice such as certified nurse midwife(CNM); Nurse practitioner (NP); Certified registered nurse anesthetist (CRNA) or clinical nurse specialists (CNS) Licensed physician assistants for impairments within his or her licensed scope of practice only. [6]

Durational Severity

Once you have established a severe impairment, you must show durational severity, which means demonstrating that you have one or more impairments that have lasted (or are expected to last) for a continuous period of 12 months or more, or that are expected to

---

[6] C.F.R. § 404.1502.

result in death. You may still apply even if you have not yet been disabled for a full 12 months, provided that your providers anticipate that your condition will meet this duration requirement.[7] SSA will use all evidence from your objective medical evidence (including other treating sources that are not considered accepted medical sources), and nonmedical sources to show the severity of your impairment and how it affects your ability to work. Non-medical sources include, but are not limited to: your testimony both written and verbal; educational personnel, prior co-workers or employers; vocational assessments; social welfare agencies, family members. [8]

Vocational Severity

The final requirement is vocational severity. Your impairment must significantly limit your ability to perform what the Social Security Administration (SSA) refers to as "substantial gainful activity" (SGA).

---

[7] You can still apply even if you have not yet been disabled for a full 12 months if your doctors expect your disability is expected to last for 12 months or more.

[8] C.F.R. § 404.1513.

SGA is a measure of work and earnings, assessing both the nature and level of your work.

- **"Substantial"** indicates that the work involves significant physical or mental efforts, even if you are working part-time, earning more, or working fewer hours with reduced responsibilities.
- **"Gainful"** means that the work is typically performed for pay or profit. Importantly, the SSA may also consider unpaid work as gainful if the tasks are generally done in a paid role. For example, small business owners who may not earn much profit but still work full-time could be considered to meet this criterion. [9]

If your disability prevents you from performing any type of work at all on a full-time level, or are earning over substantial gainful activity dollar amount defined by SSA (2025 will be over $1,620 per month gross), even a job where you would sit down to work, you are considered disabled under both SSI and SSDI.

---

[9] C.F.R. § 404.1572.

Financial Eligibility: The Non-Medical Requirements For SSI & SSDI

In addition to medical qualifications, SSA evaluates non-medical requirements for both SSDI and SSI, which differ significantly between the programs.

For SSDI, non-medical requirements are primarily determined by your work credits, earned through your contributions to Social Security. *How are work credits calculated?* Work credits are given per quarter (four times a year) and are based on how much you have contributed to Social Security Insurance through your income. 20 of those credits must be from the last 10 years of your employment, prior to your disability. You can find this info on the My Social Security portal at **ssa.gov**. 20 CFR §§ 404.110-404.115

What is interesting about SSDI is that it is based solely on what you have paid into the system through payroll taxes, not assets. This means that if you qualify as being disabled and have paid into the system, you could own a boat, have a million dollars in a 401(k), and still be eligible for SSDI benefits.

SSI's non-medical requirements, on the other hand, are asset-based. To be eligible for SSI as an individual, you must meet income/resource requirements and citizen requirements. You cannot have more than $2,000 in resources – and the SSA will consider your resources in full. (This means that your spouse's income and assets could impact your eligibility.) However, you are entitled to a home and one vehicle that is not included in your asset calculation. Generally speaking, if you are disabled, would qualify for EBT or food stamps in your state, have less than $2,000 in the bank, and have few, if any, resources, you would likely be eligible to apply for SSI.[10]

Working While Receiving Disability Benefits

It's common for people to start out working full-time as their condition worsens, eventually reducing their hours until they're just barely managing to stay employed, often because they need health insurance or financial stability. Many people assume that to collect

---

[10] 20 C.F.R. § 416.202.

SSI, you must be completely out of work. Fortunately, that's not the case.

You can work while collecting SSI or SSDI benefits, as long as you don't earn more than what's considered *substantial gainful activity* (SGA). For 2025, the SGA limit is approximately $1,620 per month. So, if your disability is making it increasingly difficult to earn a living and your working hours have been reduced, it may be time to consider applying for these benefits. The key is that your earnings stay below the SGA limit, allowing you to receive SSI/SSDI while still maintaining some level of employment.

The Role Of The Social Security Administration (SSA) In SSD Claims

In short, the Social Security Administration is involved in the claims process in every aspect, at every step. Social Security has its own legal system, its own set of rules and regulations, and its own standards for processing and hearing claims. In many ways, it's a bit similar to tax court. When you go to tax court, you don't go to a local or federal courthouse, but to a special court run and overseen by the IRS with its own rules and regulations. The Social Security court is similarly unique.

Also unlike state or federal court systems, this process is designed to be *non-adversarial*. In other words, you won't be on trial, and there are no attorneys working for Social Security that you will go up against. What's more, there is no discovery process, although it will be up to you to provide SSA with all of the evidence pertinent to your case.

There are also no formal rules of evidence. In that, there will not be anyone objecting to questions or evidence offered. Nonetheless, you should still be aware that the SSA employee who reviews your case is not a neutral judge deciding between two parties. Rather, they are an employee of the SSA and are going by the assumption that you are not disabled until you can prove otherwise.

Along the way, you need to keep in mind that the Social Security claims process is not simple. This is rather different from filing an insurance claim after damage to your car or house. Other kinds of insurance claims can be fairly straightforward and easy to get approved. Social Security, on the other hand, can be an uphill battle.

In 2023, SSA published its approval rates nationwide, which reflects consistency over prior years. At the initial application stage, SSA denied 61% of claims. At the next level of appeal, Reconsideration, SSA denied 85% of claims, and after a hearing with an administrative law judge, 30% were denied, 35% were dismissed, and only 45% were approved.

As an attorney who has practiced in many jurisdictions in the United States, and represented thousands of claimants, these numbers are consistent with each jurisdiction in which I have worked. Usually, I find that those who are truly disabled under Social Security's rigorous rules, will have no choice but to appeal over and over, as they can't work in any capacity and have no other options but to keep fighting.

At these insanely low numbers of approval rates, you have to be prepared for the fact that the claims process is both complicated and lengthy - and the burden of proving that you are truly disabled and unable to work full-time is ultimately on you. Because of this, it's important to prepare your case with the help of an attorney and work proactively to show that you qualify for the benefits you need and deserve.

BONUS RESOURCES

FAQ: SOCIAL SECURITY DISABILITY AT A GLANCE

What is Social Security Disability (SSD)?

Social Security Disability is a federal program that provides income to individuals who are unable to work due to a disability.

What is the difference between Supplemental Security Income (SSI) and Social Security Disability Insurance (SSDI)?

Both programs provide monthly income to those declared "disabled," and the medical definition of disability is the same for both SSI (Title XVI) and SSDI (Title II).

However, each program has different non-medical criteria that must be met before a medical determination can be made.

What type of disability benefits should I apply for?

The type of benefits you should apply for depends on your work history. You can apply for both SSI and SSDI, but the benefits do not stack.

What are the requirements to qualify for SSI and SSDI?

To qualify for either SSI or SSDI, you must meet the following:

- **Medical:** You must have a qualifying medical disability.
- **Durational:** Your disability must last or be expected to last for at least 12 months.
- **Vocational:** Your disability must prevent you from performing any substantial gainful activity (SGA).

What are the non-medical requirements for SSDI benefits?

To be eligible for SSDI benefits, you must have "disability insured status." This typically means having 20 quarters of coverage in the 40-quarter period prior to the onset of your disability (generally 20 credits within the past 10 years).

Claimants who became disabled before age 31 need fewer quarters of coverage. You can check your Social Security account to see how many credits you have.

What are the non-medical requirements for SSI benefits?

To qualify for SSI benefits, you must meet the following criteria:

- Have limited income and resources (no more than $2,000 in assets)
- Meet citizenship requirements

- Be under a qualifying disability

What is the role of the Social Security Administration (SSA) in the SSD claims process?

The SSA oversees the SSD claims process and has its own legal system governed by federal law, rules, and regulations. This process is similar to Tax Court, with its own claims appeal system, including hearings and reviews.

While the process is intended to be non-adversarial, SSA decision-makers are not neutral. They assume you are not disabled unless you prove otherwise. This makes it essential to be well-prepared and detailed in your case.

CHAPTER TWO:

PREPARING FOR YOUR INITIAL APPLICATION

What You Will Need To Apply For SSDI

When applying for Social Security Disability, there are several pieces of information you will need to gather. First and foremost, you'll need to provide your Social Security Number, as well as details about your work history. While Social Security already has a record of your employment and earnings, it's helpful to provide a list of your employers from at least the past five years, including part-time jobs.

If you are self-employed, you'll need to provide information about your self-employment history, including how long you've been self-employed and how much you've earned. SSA will want to know about the jobs you performed over the past 5 years before your onset of disability. You will need to describe the activities of the job, such as how long you had to stand, sit, lift etc.

SSA will ask that you fill out a form 3368.[11] This can be done in person or online. You will need information about your spouse, including their Social Security Number and any details about past marriages, if applicable. It helps to have your children's personal and Social Security information ready, as well. You will want to provide the contact information of someone that you trust that SSA can get in touch with about your application.

Next, you will be asked about your disabilities. You will need to give a list of each diagnosis that limits your ability to work. When SSA asks how your

[11] This form is available at the end of this chapter.

medical condition would affect your ability to work, this is where you describe your symptoms, and how it affected your work, thus causing you to leave work and file for disability. To this end, it's important to come to the application process with a doctor's firm diagnosis of your condition whenever possible.

Beyond this, the SSA will also need to know the date you became unable to work, or reduced your hours below SGA. Of course, this can be tricky if you've been working part-time or dealing with a long-term condition that has worsened over time. The rule of thumb in these cases is generally this: Your ***onset date*** is the date you were no longer able to earn more than *substantial gainful activity* (SGA).[12] For many, this will be the date they stopped working, but if you continued to work at reduced hours, it may be the day that you realized you could no longer work full-time.

You will also need to list your medical and mental health providers who have been treating you since you became disabled (unable to work SGA). You

---

[12] In 2025, SGA is defined as earning $1,620 per month.

should come prepared with the name of the provider, the facility they work for, what they treat you for, and their contact information. Oftentimes, it is helpful to go to your health providers' "My Chart" to pull dates of visits because the SSA will ask about the first date and last date you were seen by a medical provider. If any tests or imaging were ordered for you since your onset, it would be important to list the dates of those tests and who ordered them. (Such as an MRI, blood test, psychological evaluation etc).

If you have recently, or are receiving any other type of benefits that may have medical information for you, you will need to provide that to SSA. This can include information from workers' compensation, the Department of Veterans Affairs, attorneys, insurance companies, and vocational rehabilitation agencies.

It's important to note that the SSA will not pay benefits retroactively for more than one year prior to your application date. This means there's no need to prove your disability started years ago if the SSA won't pay for that time anyway unless you have a *date last insured* that requires you to prove an earlier disability onset. Even in this scenario, you will only get paid 1 year prior to your application date (but still need to prove disability prior to your DLI). Defining your date last insured and understanding its significance is crucial early in the process.

A Helpful Tip

The most important thing you can do is talk to your doctors and get medical help as soon as possible. Medical documentation is crucial, so the more formal evidence of your disability that you have from a doctor, the better.

Ideally, your medical provider should diagnose your disability, give medical explanations as to what is causing your symptoms, and be supportive of your application. That being said, *don't panic if you don't have this evidence on hand when you apply*. As more information is collected in the form of medical files, X-rays, MRIs, and other data, you'll be able to add evidence to your case as you go.

The disability application process can be very lengthy. So, in some cases, it is better to file early and build your case over time rather than waiting until everything is in perfect order. As long as you are receiving treatment, have a current diagnosis, and can provide the necessary information about your medical providers, you can apply and continue adding to your claim as you go through the process.

Bonus Resources

Form SSA-3368

Form **SSA-3368-BK** (06-2024) UF
Discontinue Prior Editions
Social Security Administration

OMB No. 0960-0579

DISABILITY REPORT - ADULT

PLEASE READ THIS INFORMATION BEFORE COMPLETING THIS REPORT

The office that makes the disability decision on your case will use the information you provide in this report to decide whether you are disabled. Please complete as much of the report as you can.

You may be able to apply online at: www.ssa.gov/apply.

WHAT WE MEAN BY "DISABILITY"

"Disability" under Social Security is based on your inability to work. For purposes of this claim, we want you to understand that "disability" means you are unable to work as defined by the Social Security Act. You will be considered disabled if you are unable to do any kind of work for which you are suited and if your disability is expected to last (or has lasted) for at least a year or is expected to result in death. So when we ask "when did you become unable to work," we are asking when you became disabled as defined by the Social Security Act.

IF YOU NEED HELP

You can get help from other people, such as a friend or family member. **Please do not ask your healthcare provider to complete this report.** If you cannot complete the report, you may contact us at 1-800-772-1213 (TTY 1-800-325-0778). A Social Security Representative will assist you. Have the information available from the bulleted items below when you call us. If you have an appointment, please have the information available, or the completed report ready when we contact you. If we ask you to do so, please mail the completed report to us ahead of time. **If you cannot speak or understand English, we will provide an interpreter free of charge.**

YOUR MEDICAL RECORDS

YOU DO NOT NEED TO ASK DOCTORS OR HOSPITALS FOR ANY MEDICAL RECORDS. If you have consented to us obtaining medical records from your providers, we will request your records directly from them. The information that you give us on this report tells us where to request your medical and other records.

WHAT YOU NEED TO COMPLETE THIS REPORT

- Names, addresses, and phone numbers of two people (other than your doctors) we can contact who know about your medical condition(s) and can help with your case, if needed.
- Information about any education you have completed.
- Information about all the jobs you had in the 5 years before you became unable to work.
- Any prescription or non-prescription medicines you take.
- Names, addresses, and phone numbers of any healthcare providers and information about the medical treatment you received, or testing performed.
- If you cannot remember information about your healthcare providers, the treatment you received, or the testing performed, you may be able to get that information from the telephone book, the Internet, an online medical chart, medical bills, prescriptions, or prescription medicine containers.
- If you cannot remember exact dates, provide the closest date you can remember.
- Name of organization(s) we can contact that would have medical information about your condition(s), such as Department of Veterans Affairs, social services agencies, vocational rehabilitation agencies, welfare agencies, attorneys, prisons, workers' compensation, and insurance companies who have paid you disability benefits.
- Information about any vocational rehabilitation, employment, or other support services if you are receiving Supplemental Security Income (SSI).
- **ANSWER EVERY QUESTION,** unless the report indicates otherwise: Provide as much detail as possible. If you do not know an answer, or the answer is "none" or "does not apply," please write "don't know," or "none," or "does not apply."
- Be sure to explain an answer if the question asks for an explanation, or if you want to provide additional information. If you need more space to answer any question, use **Section 11 - Remarks**.

HOW TO SUBMIT THIS REPORT

Send or bring this completed report to your local Social Security office. If you have internet access, you can locate your nearest Social Security office by ZIP code at www.socialsecurity.gov/locator. Our offices are also listed under U.S. Government agencies in your telephone directory, or you may call Social Security at 1-800-772-1213 (TTY 1-800-325-0778).

Privacy Act Statement
Collection and Use of Personal Information

Sections 205(a), 223(d), 1614(a), and 1631 of the Social Security Act, as amended, allow us to collect this information. Furnishing us this information is voluntary. However, failing to provide all or part of the information may prevent an accurate and timely decision on any claim filed.

We will use the information to determine eligibility for benefits. We may also share your information for the following purposes, called routine uses:

- To applicants, claimants, prospective applicants or claimants, other than the data subject, and their authorized representatives or representative payees to the extent necessary to pursue Social Security claims and to representative payees when the information pertains to individuals for whom they serve as representative payees, for the purpose of assisting SSA in administering its representative payment responsibilities under the Act and assisting the representative payees in performing their duties as payees, including receiving and accounting for benefits for individuals for whom they serve as payees; and
- To contractors and other Federal agencies, as necessary, for the purpose of assisting the Social Security Administration (SSA) in the efficient administration of its programs.

In addition, we may share this information in accordance with the Privacy Act and other Federal laws. For example, where authorized, we may use and disclose this information in computer matching programs, in which our records are compared with other records to establish or verify a person's eligibility for Federal benefit programs and for repayment of incorrect or delinquent debts under these programs.

A list of additional routine uses is available in our Privacy Act Systems of Records Notice (SORN) 60-0089, entitled Claims Folders System, as published in the Federal Register (FR) on April 1, 2003, at 68 FR 15784, and 60-0320, entitled Electronic Disability Claim File, as published in the FR on December 22, 2003, at 68 FR 71210. Additional information, and a full listing of all of our SORNs, is available on our website at www.ssa.gov/privacy.

Paperwork Reduction Act Statement

This information collection meets the requirements of 44 U.S.C. § 3507, as amended by section 2 of the Paperwork Reduction Act of 1995. You do not need to answer these questions unless we display a valid Office of Management and Budget control number. We estimate that it will take about 80 minutes to read the instructions, gather the facts, and answer the questions. **SEND OR BRING THE COMPLETED FORM TO THE OFFICE THAT REQUESTED IT. You can find your local Social Security office through SSA's website at www.socialsecurity.gov. Offices are also listed under U. S. Government agencies in your telephone directory or you may call Social Security at 1-800-772-1213 (TTY 1-800-325-0778).** You may send comments regarding this burden estimate or any other aspect of this collection, including suggestions for reducing the burden to: SSA, 6401 Security Blvd, Baltimore, MD 21235-6401. ***Send only comments relating to our time estimate or any other aspects of this collection to this address, not the completed form.***

AFTER COMPLETING THIS REPORT, REMOVE THIS SHEET AND KEEP IT FOR YOUR RECORDS

DISABILITY REPORT ADULT	For SSA Use Only- Do not write in this box. Related SSN Number Holder

Anyone who makes or causes to be made a false statement or representation of material fact for use in determining a payment under the Social Security Act, or knowingly conceals or fails to disclose an event with an intent to affect an initial or continued right to payment, commits a crime punishable under Federal law by fine, imprisonment, or both, and may be subject to administrative sanctions.

SECTION 1 - INFORMATION ABOUT YOU

When a question refers to "you" or "your," it refers to the person who is applying for disability benefits. **If you are completing this report for someone else,** provide information about them.

1.A. NAME (First, Middle Initial, Last, Suffix)	**1.B.** SOCIAL SECURITY NUMBER
Jane S Doe	000-00-0000

1.C. Have you used any other names on your medical or educational records? Examples include maiden name, other married names, other names, or nickname. ☒YES ☐NO

If YES, please list names used: Jane S Smith

1.D. MAILING ADDRESS (Street or PO Box) Include apartment number, if applicable.

2432 Homestreet Way

CITY	STATE/Province	ZIP/Postal Code	COUNTRY (If not USA)
MYTown	OR	12345	

1.E. EMAIL ADDRESS

myhomeemail@provider.com

1.F. DAYTIME PHONE NUMBER(S) where we can call to speak with you or leave a message, if needed. Include area code or IDD and country code if outside the USA or Canada.

Primary: (000) 000-0000 Secondary: (if available)

1.G. Can you speak and understand English? ☒YES ☐NO

If NO, what language do you prefer?

If you cannot speak and understand English, we will provide an interpreter, free of charge.

1.H. Can you read and understand English? ☒YES ☐NO

1.I. Can you write more than your name in English? ☒YES ☐NO

SECTION 2 - CONTACTS

Is there someone we can contact who can help with your claim, if needed? Examples include a family member, friend, or neighbor.

☒YES Please provide the names of two people **(other than your doctors)** we can contact who know about your medical condition(s) and can help you with your claim and can help us reach you if you become unavailable.

☐NO **We recommend that you provide at least one contact, if available.** Providing the name of someone who knows you may help us to make a decision on your claim.

2.A. NAME (First, Middle Initial, Last)	**2.B.** Relationship to the Person in **1.A.**
John R Spouse	Spouse

2.C. MAILING ADDRESS (Street or PO Box) Include apartment number, if applicable.

Same as above

CITY	STATE/Province	ZIP/Postal Code	COUNTRY (if not USA)

2.D. DAYTIME PHONE NUMBER (as described in **1.F.** above)

(111) 111-1111

SECTION 2 - CONTACTS (continued)

2.E. Can this person speak and understand English? ☒YES ☐NO

If NO, what language is preferred?

2.F. NAME (First, Middle Initial, Last)	**2.G.** Relationship to the Person in **1.A.**

2.H. MAILING ADDRESS (Street or PO Box) Include apartment number, if applicable.

CITY	STATE/Province	ZIP/Postal Code	COUNTRY (if not USA)

2.I. DAYTIME PHONE NUMBER (as described in **1.F.** above)

2.J. Can this person speak and understand English? ☐YES ☐NO

If NO, what language is preferred?

SECTION 3 - MEDICAL INFORMATION

3.A. Separately list each physical and/or mental condition that limits your ability to work. If you have cancer, please include the type and stage.

1. Degenerative Disc Disease of lower back
2. Fibromyalgia
3. Depression
4. Anxiety
5.

If you need more space, go to Section 11

3.B. What is your height? 5 feet 9 inches OR ____ centimeters

3.C. What is your weight? 180 pounds OR ____ kilograms

SECTION 4 - WORK ACTIVITY

4.A. Are you currently working?

☐NO, I have never worked (Go to question **4.B.**)

☒NO, I have stopped working (Go to question **4.C.**)

☐YES, I am currently working (Go to question **4.F.**)

IF YOU HAVE NEVER WORKED:

4.B. When do you believe your conditions(s) became severe enough to keep you from working (even though you have never worked)? (MM/DD/YYYY) ____________ (Go to **Section 5**)

IF YOU HAVE STOPPED WORKING:

4.C. When did you stop working? (MM/DD/YYYY) 07/20/2024

Why did you stop working?

☒ Because of my condition(s).

☐ Because of other reasons.

Please explain why you stopped working. Examples include laid off, early retirement, seasonal work ended, or business closed.

Even though you stopped working for other reasons, when do you believe your conditions(s) became severe enough to keep you from working? (MM/DD/YYYY) ____________

SECTION 4 - WORK ACTIVITY (continued)

4.D. Did your condition(s) cause you or your employer to make changes in your work activity? Examples include job duties, hours, or rate of pay.

☐ NO (Go to **Section 5**)

☒ YES, When did the changes start? (MM/DD/YYYY) 05/01/2024

4.E. Since the date in **4.D.** above, have you had earnings greater than $1,550 before tax in any month? Do not count sick leave, vacation, or disability pay. (We may contact you for more information.)

☐ YES (Go to **Section 5**) ☒ NO (Go to **Section 5**)

IF YOU ARE CURRENTLY WORKING:

4.F. Has your condition(s) caused you or your employer to make changes in your work activity? Examples include job duties, hours, or rate of pay.

☐ YES When did the changes start? (MM/DD/YYYY) ____________

☐ NO When did your condition(s) first start bothering you? (MM/DD/YYYY) ____________

4.G. Since your condition(s) first bothered you, have you had earnings greater than $1,550 before tax in any month? Do not count sick leave, vacation, or disability pay. (We may contact you for more information.)

☐ YES ☒ NO

SECTION 5 - EDUCATION, TRAINING, AND LITERACY

5.A. Select the highest level of school completed, including homeschooling, online education, and education received in another country.

0	K	1	2	3	4	5	6	7	8	9	10	11	12	GED	College: 1	2	3	4 or more
☐	☐	☐	☐	☐	☐	☐	☐	☐	☐	☐	☐	☐	☒	☐	☐	☐	☐	☐

Date completed: 06/1996
MM/YYYY

Name of school: MyHighSchool

City: Hometown State/Province: CA Country (if not USA): ____________

5.B. Were you in special education? ☒ NO (Go to **5.C.**) ☐ YES (Complete below)

Dates from: ____________ to ____________
MM/YYYY MM/YYYY

If YES, select the last grade you were in special education.

Pre K	K	1	2	3	4	5	6	7	8	9	10	11	12
☐	☐	☐	☐	☐	☐	☐	☐	☐	☐	☐	☐	☐	☐

Reason(s) for special education: ____________

The school where you were last in special education:

☐ Same as **5.A.**

☐ If different from **5.A.**, complete below.

Name of school: ____________

City: ____________ State/Province: ____________ Country (if not USA): ____________

SECTION 5 - EDUCATION, TRAINING, AND LITERACY (continued)

5.C. Have you received any type of **training** (specialized job, trade, or vocational training)?

☒ NO (Go to **5.D.**) ☐ YES (Complete the table below.)

NAME OF TRAINING FACILITY			PHONE NUMBER
ADDRESS			
CITY	STATE/Province	ZIP/Postal Code	COUNTRY (if not USA)
TYPE OF PROGRAM		Date Completed (or scheduled to be completed) MM/YYYY	

5.D. What written language do you use every day in most situations (at home, work, school, in community, etc.)?

English

5.E. READING - In the language you identified in **5.D.**, can you read a simple message, such as a shopping list or short and simple notes? ☒ YES ☐ NO

5.F. WRITING - In the language you identified in **5.D.**, can you write a simple message, such as a shopping list or short and simple notes? ☒ YES ☐ NO

SECTION 6 - WORK HISTORY
(If you need more space, use Section 11)

6.A. Did you have a job in the 5 years before you became unable to work because of your medical conditions?

☐ NO (Go to **Section 7**) ☒ YES (Complete the table below.)

List all the jobs you had in the 5 years before you became unable to work because of your medical conditions:

- List your most recent job first
- List all job titles even if they were for the same employer
- **Do not include jobs you held less than 30 calendar days**
- Include self-employment (e.g., rideshare driver, hair stylist)
- Include work in a foreign country

	Job Title (e.g., Cashier)	Type of Business (e.g., Grocery Store)	Dates Worked		Hours per Day	Days per Week	Rate of Pay	
			From: MM/YYYY	To: MM/YYYY			Amount	Frequency (per) hour, day, week, month, or year
1.	Barista	Coffee Shop	06/2022	07/2024	8	5	$19	HOUR
2.	Server	Restaurant	01/2022	06/2022	8	5	$18	Hour
3.	Products assembler	Manufacturer	01/2019	01/2022	8	5	$17	Hour
4.								
5.								

SECTION 6 - WORK HISTORY (continued)

Check the box below that applies to you.

☒ **I had more than one job.** (If you had more than one job, we may contact you for more information. **Do not** answer the questions in **Section 6.B** through **6.D**. Go to **Section 7**.)

☐ I had **only one job**. (If you had only one job, complete the questions in **6.B.** through **6.D.**)

6.B. Information about your work

6.B.1. For the job you listed in **6.A.**, describe in detail the tasks you did in a typical workday. Examples of tasks include stocking shelves, greeting customers, scheduling appointments, or maintaining records.

Took orders, greeted customers, prepared food and drinks, cleaned area, stocked shelves.

6.B.2. If any of the tasks listed above involved writing or completing reports, describe the type of report you wrote or completed and how much time you spent on it per workday or workweek.

N/A

6.B.3. If any of the tasks listed above involved supervising others, describe who or what you supervised and what supervisory duties you had. Examples of supervisory duties include evaluating employee job performance, making schedules, or maintaining time records.

I supervised 2 people. I would make schedules and maintain time records

6.B.4. List the machines, tools, and equipment you used regularly when doing this job and explain what you used them for. Examples of equipment include computer, telephone, forklift, air compressor, or meat slicer.

Coffee grinder and expresso machine.

6.B.5. Did this job require you to interact with coworkers, the general public, or anyone else? ☒ YES ☐ NO

If YES, **describe** who you interacted with, the purpose of the interaction, how you interacted, and how much time you spent doing it per workday or workweek. Examples include answering customer questions on the telephone for 5 hours per day or showing clients sale properties in person for 4 hours per day.

8 hours per day I would interact with the public and co-workers.

SECTION 6 - WORK HISTORY (continued)

6.C. Physical and environmental requirements of your work

Tell us how much time you spent doing the following physical activities in a typical workday. The total hours/minutes for standing, walking, and sitting should equal the Hours per Day reported in **6.A.** The example below shows an 8-hour workday with 2 hours standing and walking and 6 hours sitting (8 hours total).

Activity	How much of your workday? (Hours/Minutes)	Example:
Standing and walking (combined)	8	2 hours
Sitting	0	6 hours
Stooping (i.e., bending down & forward at waist)	20 minutes	15 minutes
Kneeling (i.e., bending legs to rest on knees)	5 minutes	15 minutes
Crouching (i.e., bending legs & back down & forward)	15 minutes	None
Crawling (i.e., moving on hands and knees)	0	None
Using fingers to touch, pick, or pinch (e.g., using a mouse, keyboard, turning pages, or buttoning a shirt): ☐ One Hand ☒ Both Hands	2 hours	2 hours (both hands)
Using hands to seize, hold, grasp, or turn (e.g., holding a large envelope, a small box, a hammer, or water bottle): ☐ One Hand ☒ Both Hands	6 hours	1 hour (both hands)
Reaching at or below the shoulder: ☐ One Arm ☒ Both Arms	1 hour	1 hour (both arms)
Reaching overhead (above the shoulder): ☐ One Arm ☒ Both Arms	10 minutes	None
Climbing stairs or ramps	0	None
Climbing ladders, ropes, or scaffolds	0	None

If you need more space, use **Section 11**

Tell us about lifting and carrying in this job. Explain what you lifted, how far you carried it, and how often you did it in a typical workday.

I would lift and carry gallons of milk sporadically throughout the day, boxes of coffee products once a day.

Select the **heaviest** weight lifted:

☐ Less than 1 lb. ☐ Less than 10 lbs. ☐ 10 lbs. ☒ 20 lbs.
☐ 50 lbs. ☐ 100 lbs. or more ☐ Other

Select the weight **frequently** lifted (i.e., 1/3 to 2/3 of the workday):

☐ Less than 1 lb. ☒ Less than 10 lbs. ☐ 10 lbs. ☐ 25 lbs.
☐ 50 lbs. or more ☐ Other 2/3 of work day

Did this job expose you to any of the following? Check all that apply.

☐ Outdoors ☒ Extreme heat (non-weather related) ☐ Extreme cold (non-weather related)
☐ Wetness ☐ Humidity ☐ Hazardous substances
☐ Moving mechanical parts ☐ High, exposed places ☐ Heavy vibrations
☐ Loud noise ☐ Other

If one or more boxes are checked, tell us about the exposure(s) and how often you were exposed.

Exposed to hot water and coffee

SECTION 6 - WORK HISTORY (continued)

6.D. Explain how your medical conditions would affect your ability to do this job.

With back pain, I can no longer stand more than 20 minutes at a time before I need to sit, laydown, or walk around. My fibromyalgia pain travels to different parts of my body. I have frequently flareups of swelling and pain in my hands or legs that make it difficult to sit or stand for very long; Repetitive use of my hands is limited to only a few minutes during a flare. Brain fog from fibromyalgia, I am unable to focus and lose attention frequently. When in a flare,I need extra breaks at work and often miss work for a few days.This happens at least twice per month. Depression and anxiety make it difficult to be around other people without experiencing panic attacks or disregulated moods.

SECTION 7 - MEDICINES

7. Are you currently taking any prescription or non-prescription medicine(s)?

☐ NO (Go to **Section 8**)

☒ YES (Complete the information below. You may need to look at your medicine containers.)

NAME OF MEDICINE	IF PRESCRIBED, GIVE DOCTOR NAME (IF KNOWN)	REASON FOR MEDICINE (IF KNOWN)
XYZ	Dr PCP	Pain
ABC	Dr Specialist	Inflammation
DEF	Dr Psychiatrist	Anxiety
GHI	Dr Psychologist	Depression

If you need to list more medicines, use **Section 11**.

SECTION 8 - MEDICAL TREATMENT

8.A. Have you seen or received treatment from a healthcare provider (doctor, hospital, clinic, psychiatrist, nurse practitioner, therapist, physical therapist, or other medical professional), or **do you have a future appointment scheduled**?

☐ NO (Go to **Section 9**)

☒ YES (Complete the chart(s) below)

You may find this information on medical bills, online medical chart, or the Internet.

8.A.1.

NAME OF FACILITY OR OFFICE	NAME OF HEALTHCARE PROVIDER THAT TREATED YOU
Make Me Well Clinic	Dr PCP

What medical conditions were treated or evaluated?
Back pain, fibromyalgia

PHONE NUMBER	DATE FIRST SEEN:	DATE LAST SEEN:	DATE OF NEXT APPOINTMENT: (IF KNOWN)
(001) 002-0033	01/2022 MM/YYYY	08/2024 MM/YYYY	10/2024 MM/YYYY

ADDRESS
123 Dr Corner Rd

CITY	STATE/Province	ZIP/Postal Code	COUNTRY (if not USA)
MyTOWN			

8.A.2.

NAME OF FACILITY OR OFFICE	NAME OF HEALTHCARE PROVIDER THAT TREATED YOU
MYTown Behavioral Health	Dr Psychiatrist & Dr Psychologist

What medical conditions were treated or evaluated?
Depression and Anxiety

PHONE NUMBER	DATE FIRST SEEN:	DATE LAST SEEN:	DATE OF NEXT APPOINTMENT: (IF KNOWN)
(123) 456-7890	07/2023 MM/YYYY	08/2024 MM/YYYY	09/2024 MM/YYYY

ADDRESS
543 Peaceful Dr

CITY	STATE/Province	ZIP/Postal Code	COUNTRY (if not USA)
Mytown	CA	00032	

8.A.3.

NAME OF FACILITY OR OFFICE	NAME OF HEALTHCARE PROVIDER THAT TREATED YOU
Fibromyalgia Care Center	Dr Specialist

What medical conditions were treated or evaluated?
Fibromyalgia

PHONE NUMBER	DATE FIRST SEEN:	DATE LAST SEEN:	DATE OF NEXT APPOINTMENT: (IF KNOWN)
(023)456-9780	06/2023 MM/YYYY	08/2024 MM/YYYY	10/2024 MM/YYYY

ADDRESS
142 Hilltop

CITY	STATE/Province	ZIP/Postal Code	COUNTRY (if not USA)
Mytown	CA	00032	

SECTION 8 - MEDICAL TREATMENT (continued)

8.A.4

NAME OF FACILITY OR OFFICE			NAME OF HEALTHCARE PROVIDER THAT TREATED YOU
What medical conditions were treated or evaluated?			
PHONE NUMBER	DATE FIRST SEEN: MM/YYYY	DATE LAST SEEN: MM/YYYY	DATE OF NEXT APPOINTMENT: (IF KNOWN) MM/YYYY
ADDRESS			
CITY	STATE/Province	ZIP/Postal Code	COUNTRY (if not USA)

8.A.5.

NAME OF FACILITY OR OFFICE			NAME OF HEALTHCARE PROVIDER THAT TREATED YOU
What medical conditions were treated or evaluated?			
PHONE NUMBER	DATE FIRST SEEN: MM/YYYY	DATE LAST SEEN: MM/YYYY	DATE OF NEXT APPOINTMENT: (IF KNOWN) MM/YYYY
ADDRESS			
CITY	STATE/Province	ZIP/Postal Code	COUNTRY (if not USA)

8.A.6.

NAME OF FACILITY OR OFFICE			NAME OF HEALTHCARE PROVIDER THAT TREATED YOU
What medical conditions were treated or evaluated?			
PHONE NUMBER	DATE FIRST SEEN: MM/YYYY	DATE LAST SEEN: MM/YYYY	DATE OF NEXT APPOINTMENT: (IF KNOWN) MM/YYYY
ADDRESS			
CITY	STATE/Province	ZIP/Postal Code	COUNTRY (if not USA)

If you need to list more facilities or healthcare providers, use **Section 11**.

SECTION 8 - MEDICAL TREATMENT (continued)

8.B. Did any of the healthcare providers listed in **8.A.** order any medical tests for you? Include tests already performed and scheduled in the future.

☐ NO (Go to **Section 9**)

☒ YES (Select tests from the chart below)

TEST	NAME OF HEALTHCARE PROVIDER OR FACILITY	DATE OF TEST (MM/YYYY)
Blood test (not HIV)	Fibromyalgia Center	06/2024
Breathing test		
Cardiac catheterization		
EEG (brain wave test)		
EKG (heart test)		
Hearing test		
HIV test		
Speech/language test		
Treadmill (exercise test)		
Vision test		
Psychological/IQ test	Mytown Behavorial Health	07/2024
Biopsy (list body part):		
MRI/CT scan (list body part):	Make Me Well Clinic	08/2023
X-ray (list body part):		
Other - please specify:		

If you need to list more tests, use **Section 11**.

SECTION 9 - OTHER MEDICAL INFORMATION

9. Does anyone else (other than your healthcare providers) have your medical information? Examples include Department of Veterans Affairs, social service agencies, vocational rehabilitation agencies, welfare agencies, attorneys, prisons, workers' compensation, and insurance companies who have paid you disability benefits.

☒ NO (Go to **Section 10** if you are receiving Supplemental Security Income (SSI) and have been asked to complete this report; if not, go to **Section 11**.)

☐ YES (Complete the information below)

NAME OF ORGANIZATION			PHONE NUMBER
ADDRESS			
CITY	STATE/Province	ZIP/Postal Code	COUNTRY (if not USA)
NAME OF CONTACT PERSON			CLAIM NUMBER (if any)
Date of First Contact	Date of Last Contact		Date of Next Contact (if any)
Reasons for Contacts			

If you need to list other people or organizations, use **Section 11**

COMPLETE THIS SECTION ONLY IF YOU ARE ALREADY RECEIVING SSI.

SECTION 10 - SUPPORT SERVICES

Provide information about your participation in support services, if applicable. Examples of support services can include:

- An Individualized Education Program (IEP) through a school (if a student aged 18-21)
- An individual work plan with an employment network under the Ticket to Work Program
- A Plan to Achieve Self-Support (PASS)
- An individualized plan for employment with a vocational rehabilitation agency or any other organization

10.A. Have you participated or are you participating in any support services mentioned above or any other vocational rehabilitation, employment services, or other support services to help you to go to work?

☐ YES (Complete the information below) ☐ NO (Go to **Section 11**)

10.B. FACILITY OR ORGANIZATION NAME			PHONE NUMBER
COUNSELOR, INSTRUCTOR, OR JOB COACH NAME			
ADDRESS (Street or PO Box) Include Suite, Building, etc.			
CITY	STATE/Province	ZIP/Postal Code	COUNTRY (if not USA)

SECTION 10 - SUPPORT SERVICES (continued)

10.C. Are you still participating in the plan or program? (Select answer below)

☐ YES Date began: ________ Expected completion date: ________
MM/YYYY MM/YYYY

☐ NO Date began: ________ Date stopped: ________
MM/YYYY MM/YYYY

Reason stopped: ____________________

10.D. What types of services, tests, or evaluation were provided?

Select all that apply:

☐ Vision test ☐ Psychological/IQ test ☐ Work classes ☐ Hearing test ☐ Work evaluation

☐ Other - Please explain: ____________________

If you need to list another plan or program, use **Section 11**

SECTION 11 - REMARKS

Please provide any additional information you did not give in earlier parts of this report. If you did not have enough space in the sections of this report to provide the requested information, please use this space to provide the additional information requested in those sections. Be sure to include the section and question number to which you are referring.

If you need additional space, use **Section 11 - Remarks (continued)**

SECTION 11 - Remarks (continued)

SECTION 12 - WHO IS COMPLETING THIS REPORT

Date Report Completed (MM/DD/YYYY)

Who is completing this report?

- ☒ The person listed in **1.A.**
- ☐ The person listed in **2.A.**
- ☐ The person listed in **2.F.**
- ☐ Someone else (Complete the information below)

NAME (First, Middle Initial, Last)	Relationship to the Person in **1.A.**

MAILING ADDRESS (Street or PO Box) Include the apartment number, if applicable.

CITY	STATE/Province	ZIP/Postal Code	COUNTRY (if not USA)

DAYTIME PHONE NUMBER where we may reach you or leave a message, if needed. Include the area code or IDD and country code if outside the USA or Canada.

CHAPTER THREE:

FILING THE INITIAL APPLICATION

Where To File Your Application

Today, one of the best ways to file for SSDI benefits is to apply online at **www.ssa.gov**, which offers a user-friendly question-and-answer format. This is the easiest way to apply for many people, but you can always opt to call your local Social Security Office and set up an appointment to apply in person at the office.

For SSI applications, you cannot apply online due to the financial criteria that must be met. Instead, you'll need to schedule an interview—either by phone or in person—where Social Security will evaluate your financial situation. If you're applying for both SSI and SSDI online, there's a question on the SSDI application that asks if you also intend to apply for SSI. If you answer yes, Social Security will set up an appointment for your SSI financial interview.

Unsure of where your local Social Security Office is? Simply visit **www.ssa.gov** and scroll to "Find an Office" at the bottom of the homepage. This will direct you to a portal that allows you to search by ZIP code and find the closest office to you. But be prepared: if you do call your local office to make an appointment, you'll likely be on hold for quite a while.

Five Essential Tips For Filling Out Your Application

1. **Include details on your marital status and past employment.**

Social Security will ask for information about your spouse and past employment, including any applications for benefits like workers' compensation or veterans' benefits, which may impact your case. For example, workers' compensation benefits can sometimes cause an offset to your SSDI benefits.

2. **Report your earnings after disability.**

While most of the answers on your application will be fairly easy to provide, there is one important question that tends to be confusing. Essentially, it asks, *"Did you receive any money from your employer after you became disabled?"*

Even if it is unclear at first, your answer is crucial because Social Security will review your earnings reports to ensure that your income after becoming disabled doesn't disqualify you from receiving benefits. If you received sick pay, vacation pay, or severance after your disability onset date, be sure to specify that on your application to avoid confusion.

3. **Note all of your dependents**.

If you have dependents—such as children under 18, if you are directly caring for a dependent older family member, or if you pay child support—there may be additional benefits available to you.

Be sure to include this information on your application, as it can result in increased monthly payments and provide extra financial support for your loved ones through your SSDI benefits. These additional benefits can be crucial in helping your family maintain financial stability while you are unable to work.

4. **Include accurate financial information.**

You will need to provide your banking information to receive direct deposit for any benefits awarded. It's recommended to keep this account separate from any shared or joint accounts to ensure Social Security benefits are exempt from creditors.

5. **Make sure your contact information is current.**

Provide an address, email, and cell phone number so that the SSA can get in touch if they need to. If you're couch surfing, provide an address where you can reliably collect mail or provide the address of a family member who is willing to hold your mail for you until you can pick it up.

Describing Your Disability And Symptoms

On your application, you will see a section for your remarks. However, while it may seem like an opportunity to share your point of view, it's actually best to *avoid* using this space to provide a detailed account of your disability.

Remember, 90% of the evidence used to determine your disability will come from your medical records, so keep your answers focused and concise. Instead of going into detail, simply list your diagnosis in this space – or a simple list of your symptoms if you don't have a formal diagnosis. Keep information minimal, as providing too much information will be used as testimonial evidence, and could be used against you without even realizing it, particularly if there are any inconsistencies in your statements versus what is said in your medical chart notes. Instead, allow your medical records and documents to speak for you.

Receiving An Initial Decision

After you file your application, Social Security will begin an investigation to make the initial decision on your case. On average, it will take about three to six months for the decision to come back, though this timeline can vary depending on the backlog and how quickly your local office is processing applications. It's so important to fill out the application and requested forms completely and in a timely manner, such as SSA

3368. [13] You will also be required to sign an Authorization to Release Information form (form SSA 827) for SSA to investigate your claim. Many cases are delayed for a long time just because the application was simply not complete. Beyond this initial decision, you should be prepared for the process, which could take approximately two years from the initial application through the agency-level appeals.

The Role Of An Attorney At The Beginning Of Your Claim

Many people choose to hire an attorney early in the application process to ensure that their paperwork is accurate and to help them navigate the legal process. While having an attorney from the start can be helpful, it's not always necessary if you understand the process and carefully follow the steps outlined above. The key is to be thorough, provide accurate information, and ensure the SSA has all the medical documentation needed to evaluate your claim.

---

[13] We discuss this form in Chapter Two of this book. At the end of that chapter, you can find an example of the form for your reference.

In cases of severe conditions that qualify for *Compassionate Allowances,* such as those requiring hospitalization or full-time care, a lawyer may not be necessary. If the SSA gathers the required information quickly and issues a favorable decision, your claim can be approved without the need for legal representation.

So, when is it essential to have a lawyer? An attorney becomes particularly helpful if your claim is denied. A seasoned disability benefits lawyer will know exactly what the SSA is looking for and how to present your case effectively. If you've been turned down for benefits, seek the help of an attorney (such as myself) to appeal the denial and improve your chances of success as your case progresses through the SSA's appeal process.

THE THREE KEYS TO QUALIFYING FOR BENEFITS

To qualify for disability benefits, you must prove you are disabled by the standards set by the Social Security Administration (SSA). There are three primary ways your SSDI or SSI claim can meet these requirements and be approved:

1. **Meeting A Listing**

Social Security has a list of specific impairments known as "listings." If your medical condition matches one of these listings, it is considered severe enough to warrant immediate benefits. Your eligibility will be confirmed based on your medical records, so it's important that your documentation clearly demonstrates your condition.

2. **Falling Under *Compassionate Allowance***

Compassionate allowances are granted to individuals with severe and often terminal conditions, such as stage four lung cancer. These allowances expedite the approval process to ensure benefits are provided quickly in cases where recovery is unlikely, and the need for financial assistance is urgent.

3. **Proving Disability Through Your Inability To Work**

The third way to qualify for benefits is by proving that you are unable to work due to a disability. This is typically more challenging than the first two methods, as it requires substantial evidence that your condition prevents you from performing any substantial gainful activity (SGA). If you fall into this category, it's advisable to work with an attorney, either at the initial stages of your application or when appealing a denial.

CHAPTER FOUR:

APPEALING AN SSD CLAIMS DENIAL

Step One: The Request For Reconsideration

The request for reconsideration is the first step in appealing an SSDI denial. During this phase, your file is reviewed by a different decision-maker to determine whether any mistakes were made in the initial review.

At this stage, if anything has changed since your initial application—such as new medical appointments, diagnoses, or worsening conditions—this is the time to submit updated information. An attorney can be particularly helpful here by gathering medical opinions and ensuring all relevant information is included.

Unfortunately, many reconsideration requests are denied. (85% nationally in 2023) But don't be discouraged—most cases are won at the hearing stage, where the presentation of your case becomes crucial. This is where having an attorney is essential.

Adult Function Reports

Either in the Initial or Reconsideration stages of your claim (and sometimes both), SSA will ask you to fill out an Adult Function Report (also known as SSA form 3373, found below).

This form is considered "written testimony." It will be used in evaluating your case, and whether it is consistent with other information provided in your case, including your medical evidence.

As you complete the Adult Function Report, please consider the following advice to ensure that your responses provide a comprehensive understanding of how your disability affects your daily life and limits your ability to work:

1. Be consistent.

It is important to maintain consistency in your answers on the form and in your application, in what you tell your medical providers, and in what you testify to in a hearing to provide a coherent and consistent portrayal of your limitations.

2. Answer the question presented.

A short yes or no answer followed by a short explanation is sufficient. Do not offer any additional information that is not related to the question.

3. Be accurate.

Your honest and specific responses to each question are crucial in accurately portraying the impact of your disability. Do not exaggerate your symptoms, but do not minimize your symptoms either. Consider that a decision-maker may not know how your disability affects you because they cannot step in your shoes, so be descriptive but accurate in your answers.

4. Be specific.

Providing specific examples of how your disability affects you mentally and physically will help others better understand your challenges.

5. Describe your adaptations.

Explain how you have changed your lifestyle to accommodate your disability. When asked, explain what you used to be able to do versus after your disability became severe. If you have changed your daily living activities to accommodate your disability, explaining these modifications can provide valuable insight into your daily life.

6. Paint a picture of good days vs. bad days.

It is not uncommon to have good days as well as bad days. It helps to quantify them. Describe how your ability to perform your activities of daily living is affected by whether you have a good day or a bad day.

For example, if you are asked whether you go to the grocery store, you could answer, "Yes, but only if I am having a good day; otherwise, I order food for pickup or delivery." If the question asks how often you go to the grocery store, your answer should be consistent with the number of good days you may have. "I go to the store approximately two times per month on a good day."

7. Refrain from offering unnecessary information or explanation.

While it's important to be specific, you should not provide additional details about your activities of daily living or your symptoms of disability unless they are asked for and directly relate to the questions.

8. Give examples.

Provide examples of how your disability limits your ability to work full-time. You might think back to what was happening when you reduced or left your work entirely due to your disability, and describe those limitations. If you have had worsening since you left your job, think about what might happen now if you tried to return to work, and describe those symptoms.

9. Provide organized answers to open-ended questions.

Some questions are open-ended. As discussed above, be specific, accurate, and organized. Often providing your thoughts in a list is helpful. (See: Form 3373, Question 6. Attached at the end of this chapter.)

10. Flip the answer.

If a question asks you to describe functioning without limits, flip the answer to include how the function or task is limiting.

For example:

Q: "Do you care for animals?"

A: "Yes, but only by letting them outside and occasionally feeding them. My kids have to help

with carrying the food and walking the dog because these tasks are too much for me".

Step Two: The Hearing Stage

Many people believe they can simply tell their story to a judge at their hearing and that this will be enough. In reality, the hearing is a formal legal process, and the judge is looking for specific evidence that meets the legal standards for disability. In some cases, judges may even suggest postponing the hearing so the applicant can find legal representation.

The hearing is your opportunity to present your evidence and meet your burden of proof. A well-prepared case is crucial at this stage, and it's important to involve an attorney early enough to prepare your case thoroughly. Most attorneys are hesitant to take on cases at the last minute, so having legal representation from the start is ideal.

How To Prepare For Your Hearing

If you have followed the steps we've outlined so far in the previous chapters of this book, you should have already met your burden of proof by the time you have your hearing and your testimony will align with your medical evidence and previous statements made during the initial and reconsideration stages.

However, it is critical that you have an attorney represent you before the judge. You have the right to legal representation. If you attend your hearing without a lawyer, the judge must notify you of your right and offer to postpone the hearing to allow you time to obtain representation if desired.

The judge at this level is not a neutral decision-maker. An experienced attorney can help present your evidence properly and make legal arguments that could preserve the record for appeal if necessary. Your attorney will also cross-examine you and any experts, such as medical or vocational experts, who may testify at your hearing to ensure that your testimony supports your claim.

The Role Of Your Medical Evidence

As a claimant, you and your attorney have the right to review the evidence before the hearing. Any evidence you want the judge to consider must be submitted at least five business days before the hearing. This includes updated medical records, functional capacity reports, witness statements, and legal arguments.

Your medical records should already be in good order if you've followed previous advice, so you'll mostly need to provide the most recent updates. Remember, the Administrative Law Judge (ALJ) is entitled to receive all your medical records, whether they help or hurt your case. Witness statements, especially from employers or coworkers, can be very useful if they demonstrate how your disability has impacted your ability to work.

You may bring witnesses to testify, but I often find that written statements are more effective. Witness statements allow the judge to consider their testimony without the need for cross-examination, which can sometimes weaken your case.

Presenting At Your Hearing

Each hearing typically lasts one hour. Post-pandemic, you now can choose to attend your hearing in person, by phone, or by video using Microsoft Teams. While phone hearings are an option, I recommend either in-person or video hearings. This allows the judge to see you and connect with you, which can be beneficial to your case. A video hearing can provide a more personal connection, while an in-person hearing allows the judge to observe your overall demeanor.

If you participate remotely, you must confirm that you're alone in the room and that no one else can hear the proceedings. Witnesses will join the hearing only when it's time to testify. Additionally, only the court reporter is permitted to record the hearing, so you must confirm that you are not recording the session.

During the hearing, the judge will place you and any witnesses under oath. A vocational expert may also testify to determine if there are jobs you could perform given your limitations. The court will ask your attorney about the status of the exhibits and whether any medical records are missing. If there are missing records, the court may grant an extension to obtain them—provided you or your attorney informed the court five business days before the hearing.

The Role Of Your Testimony

In most hearings, the judge will lead with questions - though some judges will prefer your attorney to take the lead and choose to ask follow-up questions. In either scenario, you can expect to be examined by both the judge and your attorney.

These questions about your testimony will be about your work history, education, and reasons for not being able to return to work. Expect questions about your daily living activities, as the judge will be trying to determine how your disability affects your ability to function at home.

THREE KEY TIPS FOR A GREAT TESTIMONY

1.) Speak to your medical record.

It's crucial that your answers align with your medical records and prior statements. You have to remember that the judge most likely knows the answers to the questions from your medical records, so consistent testimony with your medical records is critical.

2.) Say something if you are confused – and keep it succinct.

If you don't understand a question or can't remember something, speak up. Don't offer more information than necessary, and avoid rambling – answer questions directly, and then provide a brief explanation.

Remember, there are no formal rules of evidence in these proceedings. Therefore, another attorney for Social Security will not question you, and there will be no objections made by your attorney or the judge. What's more, your attorney will not be able to answer for you or to help you with your answers except through cross-examination of you. So, it is up to you to know the question asked and to testify truthfully to the best of your ability.

Example One

Q: Do you drive a car?

A: Yes, however, I am unable to drive more than a few miles before I experience anxiety, therefore, I only drive when necessary.

Example Two

Q: Do you go to the grocery store?

A: Yes, but only if I bring someone to help with the heavy items and carrying bags. If I don't have someone, then I only get a few items that I can carry myself.

3.) Keep calm and be yourself.

Throughout this process, it is okay to speak from the heart and be yourself – but remember to remain calm and respectful throughout the hearing. Do not get defensive with the judge or try to argue with them.

It is not uncommon for nerves to get to you, as well as a wave of emotions that surface during your hearing. You have had to be strong to get this far, and oftentimes, talking about everything that has happened since you became disabled is overwhelming. Judges are used to it, and it is okay to ask for a few minutes' break to take a breath. It is more important that you give clear testimony, than one that is not authentic.

Along the way, keep in mind that It's okay to take your usual medications before the hearing to help you focus, and if you need to stand or move during the hearing due to pain, let the judge know. My firm belief is: give positive vibes to the judge and you will receive them in return – that will go a long way to a positive outcome.

The Role Of Vocational Experts

Usually, near the end of your hearing, a vocational expert will be examined. This person will classify your past work that was over substantial gainful activity over five years, according to the *Dictionary of Occupational Titles*. The VE will then respond to hypothetical questions posed by the judge, which outline various limitations based on your case, and determine whether a person with those limitations could perform either your past work or any other work.

The hypothetical limitations presented by the judge are based on what they believe is relevant to your case. The VE first evaluates if someone with those limitations could perform any of your past relevant work. If not, the VE then determines whether there are other jobs available that the hypothetical person could perform.

An experienced attorney will know how to cross-examine the vocational expert to get testimony that states that there would be *no* jobs that a person could do with limitations that you have at your age, educational experience, and prior work. Providing prior vocational reports or medical function reports can also help strengthen cross-examination of these experts.

Naturally, there are many factors to Vocational and Medical expert testimony as it applies to the law and the facts in your case. At the end of expert testimony, the judge may or may not allow you or your attorney closing remarks. After that, the hearing is closed. Therefore, it is important that you have competent legal counsel who can cross-examine them to sway their opinion in your favor.

The Decision

You will not receive a decision on the day of your hearing. In some cases, a judge may inform you of how they intend to rule, but the decision is not official until the judge issues a written decision. This written decision is typically mailed to you 30 to 90 days after the hearing. (An attorney may be able to obtain notification as soon as the decision is entered).

The Administrative Law Judge (ALJ) follows a five-step sequential evaluation process to make their decision:

1.) ***Is the claimant presently, or after the alleged onset date, engaged in substantial gainful activity?*** [14]

The judge evaluates any work performed after your alleged disability onset date to determine whether it meets the SGA threshold. If your earnings exceed the

---

[14] This is the definition provided in the Decision:

At step one, the ALJ must determine whether the claimant is engaging in substantial gainful activity (20 CFR 416.920(b)). Substantial gainful activity (SGA) is defined as work activity that is both substantial and gainful. "Substantial work activity" is work activity that involves doing significant physical or mental activities (20 CFR 416.972(a)). "Gainful work activity" is work that is usually done for pay or profit, whether or not a profit is realized (20 CFR 416.972(b)). Generally, if an individual has earnings from employment or self-employment above a specific level set out in the regulations, it is presumed that she has demonstrated the ability to engage in SGA (20 CFR 416.974 and 416.975). If an individual engages in SGA, she is not disabled regardless of how severe her physical or mental impairments are and regardless of her age, education, and work experience. If the individual is not engaging in SGA, the analysis proceeds to the second step.

SGA level, the judge will assess how long you sustained that work. If it was a short-lived attempt that ended because of your disability, it may be deemed an unsuccessful work attempt and not held against you.

2.) *Does the applicant have severe impairment?* [15]

The judge assesses whether your impairment significantly limits your ability to perform basic work activities. If your impairments—whether physical or mental—are deemed severe, the analysis continues. The judge considers a combination of impairments, not just one.[16]

---

[15] This is the definition provided in the Decision: At step two, the ALJ must determine whether the claimant has a medically determinable impairment that is "severe" or a combination of impairments that is "severe" (20 CFR 416.920(c)). An impairment or combination of impairments is "severe" within the meaning of the regulations if it significantly limits an individual's ability to perform basic work activities.

An impairment or combination of impairments is "not severe" when medical and other evidence establish only a slight abnormality or a combination of slight abnormalities that would have no more than a minimal effect on an individual's ability to work (20 CFR 416.922, Social Security Rulings (SSRs) 85-28 and 16-3p). If the claimant does not have a severe medically determinable impairment or combination of impairments, she is not disabled. If the claimant has a severe impairment or combination of impairments, the analysis proceeds to the third step.

[16] 20 CFR 404.1521(a) and SSR 96-3P.

3.) Does the impairment meet or equal a listed impairment? [17]

The Code of Federal Regulations states that a claimant is considered disabled if their impairment—or combination of impairments—meets or equals an impairment found in the *Listing of Impairments.* This listing outlines various major body systems and specific conditions, describing the level of severity required to be deemed disabling based solely on medical review alone.

If your impairment does not directly match a listed condition, the SSA will determine whether your impairment—or combination of impairments—is *equivalent* to a listed impairment. To establish equivalence, medical evidence must demonstrate that

[17] This is the definition provided in the Decision: At step three, the ALJ must determine whether the claimant's impairment or combination of impairments is of a severity to meet or medically equal the criteria of an impairment listed in 20 CFR Part 404, Subpart P, Appendix 1 (20 CFR 416.920(d), 416.925, and 416.926). If the claimant's impairment or combination of impairments is of a severity to meet or medically equal the criteria of a listing and meets the duration requirement (20 CFR 416.909), the claimant is disabled. If it does not, the analysis proceeds to the next step.

your condition is equal in severity to the criteria outlined in a listed impairment, using the methods specified in the regulations.

4.) Does the claimant's impairment prevent them from performing past relevant work? [18]

Next, the ALJ must determine whether you have the residual functional capacity (RFC) to perform your past relevant work.[19] This refers to jobs you performed (either as actually performed or as generally performed in the national economy) in the past five years or five years prior to the date that disability must be established. In addition, the work must have lasted long enough for the claimant to learn to do the job.[20]

---

[18] This is the definition provided in the Decision: Before considering step four of the sequential evaluation process, the ALJ must first determine the claimant's residual functional capacity (20 CFR 416.920(e)). An individual's residual functional capacity is her ability to do physical and mental work activities on a sustained basis despite limitations from her impairments. In making this finding, the ALJ must consider all of the claimant's impairments, including impairments that are not severe (20 CFR 416.920(e) and 416.945; SSR 96-8p).

[19] 20 CFR 416.920(f).

[20] SGA (20 CFR 416.960(b) and 416.965).

Additionally, the work will not be considered past relevant work if the claimant started and stopped it in fewer than 30 calendar days.[21] If the claimant has the residual functional capacity to do her past relevant work, the claimant is not disabled. If the claimant is unable to do any past relevant work or does not have any past relevant work, the analysis proceeds to the fifth and last step.

5.) ***Is the claimant able to do any other work?*** [22]

At this step, the judge considers whether there is any other work you could perform given your RFC, age, education, and work experience. If you cannot perform any other work, you will be found disabled. If the SSA can show that other jobs exist in significant numbers in the national economy that you could perform, you may not be considered disabled.

Although the burden of proving disability generally rests on you, at the fifth step, the SSA must

---

[21] 20 CFR 416.960(b)(1)(ii).

[22] 20 CFR 416.920(g).

provide evidence that jobs exist in the national economy that you can perform, given your limitations, age, education, and work experience.[23]

The five-step evaluation process is designed to assess your ability to work based on medical and vocational evidence. However, the process is subjective, and judges sometimes make mistakes in how they evaluate evidence, leading to reversals in later appeals.

The better prepared your case is, the better your chances of being approved at the hearing stage - but it is far from uncommon to get an unfavorable decision at a hearing level unless your case demonstrates an especially clear-cut disability. In fact, only about 45% of cases are approved at a hearing level nationwide. If you receive an unfavorable decision from an ALJ, your case is not over. There is still one more level of appeal within the SSA's process, and beyond that, further litigation options exist outside the SSA's appeal system.

---

[23] 20 CFR 416.912 and 416.960(c).

Step Three: The Appeals Council Review

The appeals council review is the next step of recourse in the appeal process if you face a denial at a hearing level. Keep in mind that the appeal council does not generally review new evidence to support your disability unless this evidence came in shortly after your hearing concluded and relates back to your relevant timeline and the evidence was not seen by the judge. Rather, the council reviews the decision of the judge and determines if they incorrectly applied the facts to the law in your particular case.

It's also important to understand that appeal council reviews typically have a very low approval rate compared to a hearing. In rare cases, a case at this stage may be sent back to a judge to correct any errors, or sometimes benefits will be granted. Frankly, I've only seen this happen once in my career, and the approval and remand rate for this level of appeal is quite low. (2023 numbers are 13% remand and 1% approval).

That said, it's still crucial to file for an Appeals Council review for several key reasons. Most importantly, requesting an Appeals Council review helps keep your case active. Without this step, too much time may go by from your *date last insured*, and you may lose the ability to receive SSDI benefits entirely - so it's important to continually appeal your case, even if the chances of your success are statistically slim. Keep working at it, as going through the process of appeal keeps your options open.

Step Four: Filing Again Or Heading To Federal Court

If the Appeals Council issues a negative decision and denies your claim, your next step is either to file a new application or take your case to Federal Court.

If you and your attorney decide to re-file your case, you must present new medical evidence that demonstrates either a new diagnosis or a worsening condition. This option is only available after you've completed the Appeals Council review, which is why adhering faithfully to each step is so important.

Alternatively, you can take your case to Federal Court. In this step, you argue that the SSA judge made an incorrect legal decision. However, it's critical to note that your attorney must be licensed in the state of the Federal Court where you're filing the action. If your current attorney is not licensed at the federal level, they may be able to refer you to a qualified attorney who is licensed and willing to take your case forward as needed.

The Importance Of Working With An Attorney

Hiring an attorney who practices Social Security law can be invaluable, especially when appealing a denial. An attorney will review your file, identify missing medical records or gaps in evidence, and ensure that the Social Security Administration (SSA) has everything they need to fully evaluate your claim.

One key advantage is that most SSDI attorneys are registered with SSA, so once they are retained, SSA allows the attorney to gain access to most of your electronic file, providing a second, qualified set of eyes to monitor your case from the initial appeal through to the final stages.

This enables your lawyer to understand how your claim is progressing and to offer advice accordingly, including helping you to prepare evidence (oftentimes to overcome negative information in your file) and submit it to SSA directly through your electronic file.

The True Cost Of Working With A Social Security Disability Claims Attorney

Attorneys that represent claimants before the Social Security Administration are bound by their government-regulated fee agreements to ensure that attorneys do not charge an excessive fee for their services. SSA rules do not allow attorneys to charge claimants by the hour for work that they do before the Agency. They are restricted to a contingency fee agreement.

This means that attorneys can only charge 25% of an award of back benefits up to a fixed amount, whichever amount is less, and **only if you win your case.** SSA sometimes raises the fixed amount due to industry standards due to cost of living adjustments and increases in disability benefits. In 2026, the maximum dollar fee will be adjusted annually.

Another benefit is that Social Security typically pays lawyers who specialize in Social Security law directly from your back benefits, meaning you won't have to pay their fees directly when you do win.

This is great because it will never put your attorney in the position of being a debt collector against their own client. However, keep in mind that attorneys can charge for costs and expenses, such as retrieval of medical records if your state does not have a law that protects you from these costs for SSDI/SSI appeals.

With no financial downside and many benefits, bringing a lawyer on board early—especially when appealing a denial—is a smart decision. With that in mind, let's walk through what the appeal process looks like at each step.

Bonus Resources

Your 10-Step Guide To The SSDI & SSI Claims Process

Step 1: Seek Medical Treatment

From the very beginning of your claim, it's crucial to seek regular medical treatment and consult specialists as needed. For example:

- **Fibromyalgia**: Make sure your diagnosis is from a Fibromyalgia specialist or rheumatologist who conducts a tender point test.
- **Mental Health**: A neuropsychological evaluation from a PhD or PsyD level doctor is very beneficial.

Always discuss how your disabilities affect your daily activities with your healthcare providers. Your level of functioning is a key factor in the SSA's decision. The SSA will review your ability to function at home to assess how you might function in a job environment.

Ensure your medical records align with your testimony, both in writing and later in front of a judge.

Step 2: Keep Records And Logs

Maintain a consistent journal (at least weekly) describing how your disabilities impact your daily life. For example, if you had a particularly difficult day, note what happened, including the duration and intensity of your symptoms:

- **Example**: "On Tuesday, I woke up in pain and could only sit in a dining room chair for a few minutes before needing to lie down with an ice pack. I had to rest for two 1 ½ hour naps that day."

If you experience migraines or seizures, keep a detailed log. Document the frequency and severity, and share these logs regularly with your doctors.

Step 3: Gather Medical Evidence

By the reconsideration or hearing level, request that one of your providers complete a Residual

Functional Capacity (RFC) form, detailing your physical and mental limitations. This can be a key piece of evidence in your case.

If you're unrepresented, contact your local SSA office monthly for updates on your records. If any are missing, request them from your doctors and fax them to the SSA. You can use inexpensive efax services to make this process easier.

Step 4: Admit To SSA Examinations

The SSA may send you to their doctors for a consultative exam. These doctors aren't necessarily helpful to your case, so it's important to have regular treatment from your own specialists. Remember that SSA's doctors are evaluating you from the moment you arrive at their office. Always give your best effort and answer questions truthfully and consistently with what you've shared with your own doctors.

Step 5: Complete The Function Report

You and someone close to you may receive a Function Report, which will be used to assess your credibility against your medical records. Answer each question based on your journals, logs, and medical reports. For example:

- **Question**: "List household chores you are able to do."

  Answer: "I can do light chores like dusting, dishes, or laundry, but only in 15-minute increments due to pain. It often takes me a full day to complete one task, and I can't do heavy chores like vacuuming or yard work due to pain and fatigue."

When responding, always explain how your disability has forced you to adapt your lifestyle.

Step 6: Prepare For Your Hearing

If you've followed the guidance in earlier chapters, your medical records and testimony should align, meeting your burden of proof. However, having an attorney represent you at your hearing is critical. Your attorney can properly present your evidence, cross-examine medical and vocational experts, and protect your testimony for appeal if necessary.

Step 7: Gather And Submit Your Evidence

All evidence, including medical records, witness statements, and RFC forms, must be submitted to the judge at least five business days before the hearing. If you've followed the tips in this book, your medical record should be in good shape, and you'll only need to submit the most recent records.

Witness statements can also be helpful, particularly from prior employers or coworkers who have observed how your disabilities impacted your ability to work.

Step 8: Present At Your Hearing

You'll have the option to attend your hearing in person, via phone, or through a video call. I recommend choosing either in-person or video, as these options allow the judge to connect with you visually, which can make a difference in how they perceive your testimony.

The hearing is a closed proceeding, and the judge will place you and any witnesses under oath. During testimony, it's important to answer questions clearly, concisely, and truthfully. If you don't understand a question, ask for clarification. If you don't remember something, say so. Keep your answers short and to the point, and always stay calm and respectful.

Step 9: Obtain Vocational Testimony

A vocational expert (VE) will testify at your hearing, classifying your past work and answering hypothetical questions about your ability to work with your limitations. An experienced attorney will know how to cross-examine the VE to help build your case.

Step 10: The Decision

You likely won't receive a decision on the day of your hearing. It can take 30–60 days to receive the written decision in the mail. The SSA uses a five-step evaluation process to determine whether you qualify for benefits:

1. **Substantial Gainful Activity (SGA)**: Are you able to engage in work that earns above a certain threshold?
2. **Severe Impairment**: Does your impairment significantly limit your ability to perform basic work activities?

3. **Meeting Or Equaling A Listed Impairment**: Does your impairment meet or equal a condition listed in the SSA's Listing of Impairments?
4. **Past Relevant Work**: Can you perform any work you've done in the past five years?
5. **Ability To Do Other Work**: Considering your RFC, age, education, and work experience, can you perform other jobs available in the national economy?

If the judge makes a mistake in this process, you have the right to appeal. If you receive an unfavorable decision, it's not the end—there are still opportunities to challenge the outcome.

RFC Medical

MEDICAL OPINION RE: ABILITY TO DO WORK RELATED ACTIVITIES

(PHYSICAL) Date:

To:

RE: Patient:____

DOB: ______________________________

For each activity shown below, indicate your (1) patients ability to perform the activity; and (2) identify the medical findings that support your opinion regarding the limitations (such as physical exam findings, MRI's, lab tests, history, symptoms, etc.).

1. Nature, frequency and length of contact with your patient: ____

2. Diagnoses:____
____
____

3. Prognosis:____

4. List your patient's symptoms:____
____
____
____

5. Identify clinical findings and objective signs:
____
____
____

6. Describe treatment and response to treatment, including side effects of medications, such as drowsiness, fatigue, dizziness, nausea, memory and concentration deficits.

etc.:____

____

____

____

7. Have your patient's impairments lasted or can they be expected to last at least 12 mos?
Circle one: Yes No

8. Is it reasonable to expect that your patient would experience substantial difficulty with stamina, pain or fatigue if she or he worked full time, eight hours a day at a sedentary or light level of exertion? Circle one: Yes No

9. Would your patient likely need to work at a reduced work pace if employed full time, eight hours a day at a light or sedentary level of exertion? Circle one: Yes No

10. Would your patient's health problems be made worse if she or he worked full time, eight hours a day at a light or sedentary level of exertion? Circle one: Yes No

11. Does your patient have (a) condition(s) that can be expected to result in death?
Circle one: Yes No

12. Is your patient a malingerer? Circle one: Yes No

13. Do mental health issues contribute to the severity of your patient's symptoms and functional limitations?
Circle one: Yes No

What are the psychological conditions affecting your patient's physical condition? Circle the ones that apply:

Depression Anxiety Personality disorder PTSD Other ____________________

14. Are your patient's impairments and illness(es) consistent with causing the types of limitations she or he experiences? Circle one: Yes No

15. How often does your patient experience symptoms severe enough to interfere with her or his attention and concentration? Circle one:

Never Seldom Often Frequently Very Frequently 16. To what degree can your patient

tolerate work stress? Circle one:

Uncertain Incapable of even "low stress" jobs Capable of low stress jobs

Moderate work stress tolerable Capable of high stress work

17. Please explain the reasons for your conclusion to the question above:____

18. Does the patient have one or more impairments that requires her or him to:

a. Change position or posture more than once every two hours?
Circle one: Yes No

b. Affect her or his walking so much it interferes with the ability to independently initiate, sustain or complete normal activities of daily living?
Circle one: Yes No

c. Have sustained disturbance of gross and dexterous movements OR gait and station in two extremities?
Circle one: Yes No

19. If you answer yes to any of the above, please state what medical findings support this:____

20. What is your patient's maximum ability to stand and walk with normal breaks in an 8 hour workday:
Circle one
Less than 2 hrs About 2 hrs About 3 hrs About 4 hrs
About 6 hrs No limit

21. What is your patient's ability to sit with normal breaks in an 8 hour workday:
Circle one
Less than 2 hrs About 2 hrs About 3 hrs About 4 hrs
About 6 hrs No limit

22. If your patient must periodically alternate sitting, standing or walking to relieve discomfort:
a. How many minutes can your patient sit before changing position?
____
b. How many minutes your patient stand before changing position? ______________ c. How frequently in minutes must your patient walk around? ______________

d. How long in duration must your patient walk each time? ______________ e. Does your patient need to shift at will from sitting or standing/walking?______________ f. Will you patient need to lie down at unpredictable intervals during a work shift?
____

g. If yes, how often do you think this will happen?

____

23. What medical findings support the limitations described above?

____

____

____

____

____

____

____

____

In an average 8 hour work day, "rarely" = 0% to 5%, "occasionally"= less than 2.75 hours, "frequently"=up to 5 hours.

24. What are your patient's limitations in these functions:

	Frequently	Occasionally	Rarely	Never
Twist				
Stoop				
Crouch				
Climb stairs				
Climb ladders				

25. Are the following physical functions affected by the impairment? Circle the ones that apply
Reaching Handling Fingering Feeling Pushing/Pulling

In an average 8 hour work day, "rarely" = 0% to 5%, "occasionally"= less than 2.75 hours, "frequently"=up to 5 hours.

26. How many pounds can your patient lift and carry in a competitive workplace:

	Frequently	Occasionally	Rarely	Never
Less than 10				
10 lbs				
20 lbs				
50 lbs				

27. How are these physical functions affected?

___

___

4

28. What medical findings support this?

___

___

29. What are your patient's environmental restrictions to:

	No restriction	Avoid concentrated exposure	Avoid moderate exposure	Never
Extreme cold/heat				
Humidity				
Noise				
Fumes, odors, dust, gases, poor ventilation				
Hazards (machinery, heights)				

30. State any work-related activities which are affected by her or his impairment – such as assistive devices for ambulation, need to elevate legs, limits on kneeling, or limitations related to a mental impairment – and include the medical findings that support this:

___

___

___

___

31. On the average, how often do you anticipate that your patient's impairments or treatment would cause your patient to be absent from work? Circle one:

Never Less than once a month Once a month Twice a month

Three times a month Four or more times a month

32. If yes, is this a situation where years of past drug or alcohol abuse have resulted in ongoing health problems that will now exist even though drug or alcohol abuse may have reduced/abated?

Circle Yes or No.

33. If you are not an M.D., a Psy.D., a Ph.D, or a D.O., do you provide treatment to your patient in a clinic where a supervisory M.D., a Psy.D., a Ph.D, or D.O. is present? Circle Yes or No.

34. If you circled Yes to #33, please provide the name of the supervisory M.D., a Psy.D., a Ph.D, or D.O. who supervises your treatment of your patient: ____ 35. If you circled Yes to #33, please have your supervisory M.D., Psy.D., Ph.D. or D.O. review and sign their agreement with your opinion below.

Signature____

_ Printed/typed

name____

Address:____

____

Telephone:____
Date:____

I am the supervisory M.D./Psy.D./Ph.D. or D.O. overseeing our patient's treatment. I concur with this opinion provided by our patient's treating provider.

Signature

____

Printed/Typed name ____

RFC Mental

MENTAL IMPAIRMENT QUESTIONNAIRE
(RFC & LISTINGS)

Date

Provider's Name:_________________ Provider's Phone#__________ Patient's

Name:____________________ DOB: __________________

Please answer the following questions concerning your patient's impairments.

1. Date Treatment began:__________________

2. Frequency of Treatment (Weekly/Bi-weekly/ monthly) Date of Last Appointment: ____________ 3.

Please check the box and name on all Current Diagnoses:

☐ Neurocognitive Disorders: ____________________________
☐ Schizophrenia spectrum, and Other Psychotic Discorders ____________________
☐ Depressive, BiPolar and other Related Disorders ________________________
☐ Intellectual Disorder ____
☐ Anxiety and Obsessive-impulsive Disorders
☐ Somatic Symptom and Related Disorders ______________________________
☐ Personality and impulse-control Disorders ____________________________
☐ Autism spectrum disorder _____________
________________________ ☐ Depressive, BiPolar and other Related Disorders
__________________________ ☐ Neurodevelopmental Disorders
______________________________________ ☐ Eating Disorders
☐ Trauma and
Stress Related Disorders ________________________________

4. Has the patient's impairment lasted, or is it expected to last, at least 12 months? Yes ________ No_______

5. Check the box relating to the patient's limitations due to the above impairments

**(See Explanation attached)

Page 1

A. Understand Remember or Apply Information: ☐ None ☐ Mild ☐ Moderate ☐ Marked ☐ Extreme
B. Interact with Others: ☐ None ☐ Mild ☐ Moderate ☐ Marked ☐ Extreme
C. Concentrate Persist or Maintain Pace: ☐ None ☐ Mild ☐ Moderate ☐ Marked ☐ Extreme
D. Adapt and Manage Oneself ☐ None ☐ Mild ☐ Moderate ☐ Marked ☐ Extreme

6. Do you believe the patient is a malingerer? Yes______ No_______

7. If the medical diagnosis has been documented for over a period of at least two years,

☐ Is the medical treatment, mental health therapy, psychosocial or highly structured setting that is ongoing and that diminishes the symptoms and signs of the mental disorder **AND** ☐ Marginal adjustment, that is, the patient has minimal capacity to adapt to changes in his/her environment or to demands that are not already part of his/her daily life.

8. Is there evidence of current drug or alcohol abuse? Yes______ No______ **if** the answer is "Yes" would the impairment exist in the absence of the drug or alcohol abuse? Yes_______ No_______

9. Does the psychiatric condition exacerbate your patient's experience of pain or any other physical symptoms?

Yes_______ No_________

If Yes please explain:

10. If the patient was working full time, 8 hours a day, forty hours a week, is it likely that the patient would have substantial difficulty getting along appropriately with members of the public or co workers he/she might encounter on the job? Yes _______ No _________

11. If the patient was working full time, 8 hours a day, forty hours a week, is it likely that the patient would have substantial difficulty getting along appropriately with Supervisors?
Yes _______ No _________

To Determine your patients ability to do work-related activities on a day to day basis give us your opinion **based on your examination** but do not include patient's age, sex or work experience.

DEFINITIONS OF RATING TERMS

No Limitations: The Individual has no limitations in this area in a work setting **Mildly Limited:** The Individual would experience symptoms that would impact the ability to work full time successfully and effectively **11% to 19%** of the time in a work setting. **Moderately Limited:** The Individual would experience symptoms that would impact the ability to work full time successfully and effectively **20% to 29%** of the time in a work setting. **Markedly Limited:** The Individual would experience symptoms that would impact the ability to work full time successfully and effectively **30% to 39%** of the time in a work setting.

Page 2

Extremely Limited: The Individual would experience symptoms that would impact the ability to work full time successfully and effectively **40% or more** of the time in a work setting.

Physical and Mental
Aptitudes needed to do **No Limitations** **Mildly Limited** **Moderately** **Markedly** **Extremely** Unskilled work:

A. Remember Procedures ___

B. Understand & Remember

Simple instructions

C. Maintain Attention for 2
Hour segments

D. Maintain Regular
Attendance E. Get along w/supervisors __

F. Complete 8 hr. day without
Needs add'l rest periods __

G. Perform work without
Getting Distracted ___ 12. If awarded,

can your patient manage benefits in his or her own best interest? Yes ______ No ________

13. On the average, how often do you anticipate that your patient's impairments or treatment would cause your patient to be absent from work? (Mark one below)
_____Never _______About once a month _______About twice a month ____About three times a month
_______About Four times a month _______More than four times a month

14. Has the patient received Mental Health counseling services from a treatment team of counselors or therapists, however labeled, with a Doctoral level, M.D., D.O.; PhD.: PsyD; Ed.E or other Doctoral level person who has a Supervisory or Consultative role with the treatment team? Yes__________ No__________

Signature:___ Date:___

PRINTED/TYPED NAME:___

Address:___

Signature of supervisory doctor (MD, PhD, PsyD):___

Thank you for your valuable time and attention to this matter. If you have any questions, please feel free to contact this office.

Please see the attached Explanation of the Mental Impairment Questionnaire (Pg 1 of 2 pages)

Paragraph B criteria

• B1 - **Understand,Remember, or Apply Information**

• *the abilities to learn, recall, and use information to perform work activities* • understanding and learning terms, instructions, procedures

• following one or two step oral instructions to carry out a task

• describing work activities to someone else

• asking and answering questions and providing explanations

• a recognizing a mistake and correcting it

• identifying and solving problems

• sequencing multi-step activities

• using reason and judgment to make work-related decisions

• B2 - **interact with others**

o *the abilities to relate to and work with supervisors, coworkers, and the public* • cooperating with others

• asking for help when needed

• handling conflicts with others

• stating own point of view

• initiating or sustaining conversation

• understanding and responding to social cues (physical, verbal, emotional) • responding to requests, suggestions, criticism, correction, and challenges • keeping social interactions free of excessive irritability, sensitivity, argumentativeness, or suspiciousness

• B3 - **concentrate,persistence, or maintain pace**

o *the abilities to focus attention on work activities and stay on task at a sustained rate* • initiate and perform a task that you understand and know how to do

• working at an appropriate and consistent pace

• completing tasks in a timely manner

• ignoring or avoiding distractions while working

• changing activities or work settings without being disruptive

• working close to or with others without interrupting or distracting them

- sustaining an ordinary routine and regular attendance at work
- working a full day without needing more than the allotted number or length of rest periods during the day

Function Report -- Adult

FUNCTION REPORT - ADULT

READ ALL OF THIS INFORMATION BEFORE YOU BEGIN COMPLETING THIS FORM

IF YOU NEED HELP

If you need help with this form, complete as much of it as you can and call the phone number provided on the letter sent with the form, or contact the person who asked you to complete the form. If you need the address or phone number for the office that provided the form, you can get it by calling Social Security at 1-800-772-1213.

HOW TO COMPLETE THIS FORM

The information that you give us on this form will be used by the office that makes the disability decision on your disability claim. You can help them by completing as much of the form as you can.

It is important that you tell us about your activities and abilities.

- Print or type.
- **DO NOT LEAVE ANSWERS BLANK.** If you do not know the answer or the answer is "none" or "does not apply," please write "don't know" or "none" or "does not apply."
- Do not ask a doctor or hospital to complete this form.
- Be sure to explain an answer if the question asks for an explanation, or if you think you need to explain an answer.
- If more space is needed to answer any questions, use the "REMARKS" section on Page 10, and show the number of the question being answered.
- If a specific activity is performed with the help of others, please indicate that.

Function Report - Adult - Form SSA-3373-BK

REMEMBER TO GIVE US THE NAME AND ADDRESS OF THE PERSON COMPLETING THIS FORM ON PAGE 10

Privacy Act Statements
Collection and Use of Personal Information

Sections 205(a), 223(d), and 1631 of the Social Security Act, as amended, allow us to collect this information. Furnishing us this information is voluntary. However, failing to provide all or part of the information may prevent an accurate and timely decision on any claim filed.

We will use the information you provide to determine benefits eligibility. We may also share the information for the following purposes, called routine uses:

- To third party contacts (e.g., employers and private pension plans) in situations where the party to be contacted has, or is expected to have, information relating to the individual's capability to manage his or her benefits or payments, or his or her eligibility for entitlement to benefits or eligibility for payments, under the Social Security program; and

- To contractors and other Federal agencies, as necessary, for the purpose of assisting the Social Security Administration (SSA) in the efficient administration of its programs. We will disclose information under this routine use only in situations in which we may enter into a contractual or similar agreement to obtain assistance in accomplishing an SSA function relating to this system record.

In addition, we may share this information in accordance with the Privacy Act and other Federal laws. For example, where authorized, we may use and disclose this information in computer matching programs, in which our records are compared with other records to establish or verify a person's eligibility for Federal benefit programs and for repayment of incorrect or delinquent debts under these programs.

A list of additional routine uses is available in our Privacy Act System of Records Notices (SORN) 60-0089, entitled Claims Folders System, as published in the Federal Register (FR) on October 31, 2019, at 84 FR 58422, and 60-0320, entitled Electronic Disability Claim File, as published in the FR on June 6, 2020 at 85 FR 34477. Additional information, and a full listing of all of our SORNs, is available on our website at www.ssa.gov/privacy.

Paperwork Reduction Act Statement - This information collection meets the requirements of 44 U.S.C. § 3507, as amended by section 2 of the Paperwork Reduction Act of 1995. You do not need to answer these questions unless we display a valid Office of Management and Budget control number. We estimate that it will take about 61 minutes to read the instructions, gather the facts, and answer the questions. **SEND OR BRING THE COMPLETED FORM TO YOUR LOCAL SOCIAL SECURITY OFFICE. You can find your local Social Security office through SSA's website at www.socialsecurity.gov. Offices are also listed under U. S. Government agencies in your telephone directory or you may call Social Security at 1-800-772-1213 (TTY 1-800-325-0778).** *You may send comments regarding this burden estimate or any other aspect of this collection, including suggestions for reducing this burden to: SSA, 6401 Security Blvd, Baltimore, MD 21235-6401.* ***Send only comments relating to our time estimate or other aspects of this collection to this address, not the completed form.***

PLEASE REMOVE THIS SHEET BEFORE RETURNING THE COMPLETED FORM.

FUNCTION REPORT - ADULT

How your illnesses, injuries, or conditions limit your activities

For SSA Use Only
Do not write in this box.

Anyone who makes or causes to be made a false statement or representation of material fact for use in determining a payment under the Social Security Act, or knowingly conceals or fails to disclose an event with an intent to affect an initial or continued right to payment, commits a crime punishable under Federal law by fine, imprisonment, or both, and may be subject to administrative sanctions.

SECTION A - GENERAL INFORMATION

1. **NAME OF DISABLED PERSON** *(First, Middle Initial, Last)*	2. **SOCIAL SECURITY NUMBER**
Jane R Doe	000-00-0000

3. **YOUR DAYTIME TELEPHONE NUMBER** *(If there is no telephone number where you can be reached, please give us a daytime number where we can leave a message for you.)*

000 000-0000
Area Code *Phone Number*

☒ Your Number ☐ Message Number ☐ None

4. a. Where do you live? *(Check one.)*

☒ House ☐ Apartment ☐ Boarding House ☐ Nursing Home
☐ Shelter ☐ Group Home ☐ Other *(What?)*

b. With whom do you live? *(Check one.)*

☐ Alone ☒ With Family ☐ With Friends
☐ Other *(Describe relationship.)*

SECTION B - INFORMATION ABOUT YOUR ILLNESSES, INJURIES, OR CONDITIONS

5. How do your illnesses, injuries, or conditions limit your ability to work?

I am unable to sit for more than 15 minutes at a time without having to get up and move around or lay down; I cant use my hands repetitively more than 10 minutes at a time.

I am unable to stand or walk for more than 10 minutes at a time before I need to sit or lay down. I have to elevate my feet at waist level 2xs per day

I am unable to be around any people for more than 30 minutes without having anxiety. I don't get along with other people and have had problems with co-workers and supervisors when under stress.

SECTION C - INFORMATION ABOUT DAILY ACTIVITIES

6. Describe what you do from the time you wake up until going to bed.

Each day varies depending on whether its a good day or a bad day. On an average day, I wake up between 9:00 - 10:00 and I get a simple breakfast. I take my morning medications and do a light chore for a 10-15 minutes (put clothes in laundry or wipe countertops). Around 11:00 I go back to bed or sleep in a recliner for 1-2 hours. In the afternoon, I will

7. Do you take care of anyone else such as a wife/husband, children, grandchildren, parents, friend, other? ☒ Yes ☐ No

If "YES," for whom do you care, and what do you do for them?

2 children. I make sure they do their homework. I will give them snacks.

8. Do you take care of pets or other animals? ☒ Yes ☐ No

If "YES," what do you do for them?

Let them outside and feed them.

9. Does anyone help you care for other people or animals?

If "YES," who helps, and what do they do to help? ☒ Yes ☐ No

My kids help with bringing in food, feeding them and walking them.

10. What were you able to do before your illnesses, injuries, or conditions that you can't do now?

I used to take walks and go shopping at the mall. I used to attend my kids sport events

11. Do the illnesses, injuries, or conditions affect your sleep? ☒ Yes ☐ No

If "YES," how?

I am unable to stay asleep due to pain. I have to take sleep medication.

12. **PERSONAL CARE** (Check here ☐ if **NO PROBLEM** with personal care.)

a. Explain how your illnesses, injuries, or conditions affect your ability to:

Dress I cannot bend over to tie shoes; I can't button top

Bathe I have to use a chair in the shower

Care for hair I cannot lift my hands overhead for long. My husband helps with shampoo

Shave I do not shave legs anymore

Feed self I can feed myself

Use the toilet I can use the toilet, but need grab bar to get up and down

Other

b. Do you need any special reminders to take care of personal needs and grooming? ☐ Yes ☒ No

If "YES," what type of help or reminders are needed?

c. Do you need help or reminders taking medicine? ☒ Yes ☐ No

If "YES," what kind of help do you need?

I have to set alarm on phone to take meds or my family has to remind me.

13. MEALS

a. Do you prepare your own meals? ☒ Yes ☐ No

If "Yes," what kind of food do you prepare? (For example, sandwiches, frozen dinners, or complete meals with several courses.)

Simple meals such as sandwiches or microwave dinners or something that I can put in the slow cooker.

How often do you prepare food or meals? (For example, daily, weekly, monthly.)

I prepare my own breakfast (cereal or toast). My family helps with lunch and dinners.

How long does it take you? 15-30 minutes with breaks

Any changes in cooking habits since the illness, injuries, or conditions began?

I used to be able to cook full meals for my family.

b. If "No," explain why you cannot or do not prepare meals.

14. HOUSE AND YARD WORK

a. List household chores, both indoors and outdoors, that you are able to do. (For example, cleaning, laundry, household repairs, ironing, mowing, etc.)

light dusting, wiping down counters, I can load laundry but need help pulling the clothes out of the dryer. I can sit and fold them.

b. How much time does it take you, and how often do you do each of these things?

15 minute increments

c. Do you need help or encouragement doing these things? ☒ Yes ☐ No

If "YES," what help is needed?

Family helps with cooking, cleaning and yard work.

d. If you don't do house or yard work, explain why not.

I have too much pain to do any chores without needing to rest every 15 minutes or so.

15. GETTING AROUND

a. How often do you go outside? 1-2 xs per week

If you don't go out at all, explain why not.

b. When going out, how do you travel? *(Check all that apply.)*

☐ Walk ☐ Drive a car ☒ Ride in a car ☐ Ride a bicycle

☐ Use public transportation ☐ Other *(Explain)*

c. When going out, can you go out alone? ☐ Yes ☐ No

If "NO," explain why you can't go out alone.

Yes, but only short distances

d. Do you drive? ☐ Yes ☐ No

If you don't drive, explain why not.

I have pain in my back and hands. I also have anxiety. I don't feel safe in driving, or that I have good reaction response.

16. SHOPPING

a. If you do any shopping, do you shop: *(Check all that apply.)*

☒ In stores ☐ By phone ☐ By mail ☒ By computer

b. Describe what you shop for.

groceries, household products

c. How often do you shop and how long does it take?

In store, 15 minutes. Online- it may take 30-45 minutes in increments.

17. MONEY

a. Are you able to:

Pay bills	☒ Yes	☐ No	Handle a savings account	☒ Yes	☐ No
Count change	☒ Yes	☐ No	Use a checkbook/money orders	☒ Yes	☐ No

Explain all "NO" answers.

b. Has your ability to handle money changed since the illnesses, injuries, or conditions began? ☐ Yes ☒ No

If "YES," explain how the ability to handle money has changed.

18. HOBBIES AND INTERESTS

a. What are your hobbies and interests? (For example, reading, watching TV, sewing, playing sports, etc.)

I watch tv or read a book for short periods of time

b. How often and how well do you do these things?

I can do these for 15-30 minutes at a time with breaks

c. Describe any changes in these activities since the illnesses, injuries, or conditions began.

I used to be able to go to the movies or sit through a whole movie without needing to rest.

I used to be able to read several chapters of a book at a time.

19. SOCIAL ACTIVITIES

a. How do you spend time with others? *(Check all that apply.)*

☐ In person ☐ On the phone ☐ Email ☒ Texting ☐ Mail

☒ Video Chat (for example Skype or Facetime) ☐ Other *(Explain)*

b. Describe the kinds of things you do with others.

I talk to my family by Facetime. I text my family and friends periodically throughout the day.

How often do you do these things? Once a week for about 30 minutes. Texting periodically daily.

c. List the places you go on a regular basis. (For example, church, community center, sports events, social groups, etc.)

I no longer go to places on a regular basis. I go to doctors appointments and occasionally the grocery store

Do you need to be reminded to go places? ☒ Yes ☐ No

How often do you go and how much do you take part?

1-2xs per month

Do you need someone to accompany you? ☒ Yes ☐ No

If "YES", explain.

I need help with grocery shopping (lifting and carrying); I need help getting to my doctor appointments on time.

d. Do you have any problems getting along with family, friends, neighbors, or others? ☒ Yes ☐ No

If "YES," explain.

Due to pain, I have increased anxiety and irritability towards others.

e. Describe any changes in social activities since the illnesses, injuries, or conditions began.

I used to visit my family and friends a few times per week. I would also go to church regularly. I no longer do any of those activities.

SECTION D - INFORMATION ABOUT ABILITIES

20. a. Check any of the following items that your illnesses, injuries, or conditions affect:

- [x] Lifting
- [x] Squatting
- [x] Bending
- [x] Standing
- [ ] Reaching
- [x] Walking
- [x] Sitting
- [x] Kneeling
- [ ] Talking
- [ ] Hearing
- [x] Stair Climbing
- [ ] Seeing
- [x] Memory
- [x] Completing Tasks
- [x] Concentration
- [ ] Understanding
- [ ] Following Instructions
- [x] Using Hands
- [x] Getting Along With Others

Please explain how your illnesses, injuries, or conditions affect each of the items you checked. (For example, you can only lift [how many pounds], or you can only walk [how far])

I cannot lift more than 10 lbs. I cannot bend without pain. I can only stand for 10-15 minutes before I need to move around or lay down. I lose concentration after 10-15 minutes due to pain. I have a hard time getting along with others due to anxiety and pain.

b. Are you: [x] Right Handed? [ ] Left Handed?

c. How far can you walk before needing to stop and rest? 1/2 block

If you have to rest, how long before you can resume walking?
5 minutes

d. For how long can you pay attention? 10-15 minutes

e. Do you finish what you start? *(For example, a conversation, chores, reading, watching a movie.)* [ ] Yes [x] No

f. How well do you follow written instructions? (For example, a recipe.)
I don't follow detailed written instructions. I can follow 1-2 step instructions.

g. How well do you follow spoken instructions?
I don't follow spoken instructions very well. I tend to forget after the 1st step.

h. How well do you get along with authority figures? (For example, police, bosses, landlords or teachers.)
I do not get along with authority figures. I tend to cry or panic if I am corrected.

i. Have you ever been fired or laid off from a job because of problems getting along with other people? [x] Yes [ ] No

If "YES," please explain.
My boss told me that I was doing my job wrong and I started crying and left my shift early.

If "YES," please give name of employer.

j. How well do you handle stress?

I do not handle stress well

k. How well do you handle changes in routine?

I do not handle changes in routine well

l. Have you noticed any unusual behavior or fears? ☒ Yes ☐ No

If "YES," please explain.

I have a fear of leaving my house because I might have a panic attack.

21. Do you use any of the following? *(Check all that apply.)*

☐ Crutches	☒ Cane	☐ Hearing Aid
☐ Walker	☒ Brace/Splint	☐ Glasses/Contact Lenses
☐ Wheelchair	☐ Artificial Limb	☐ Artificial Voice Box
☐ Other (Explain)		

Which of these were prescribed by a doctor?

Yes. Cane for my back and brace for my wrists

When was it prescribed?

About 2 months ago

When do you need to use these aids?

Any time I am walking, I need to use the cane. I use the wrist brace anytime I am doing anything repetitive with my hands.

22. Do you currently take any medicines for your illnesses, injuries, or conditions? ☒ Yes ☐ No

If "YES, "do any of your medicines cause side effects? ☐ Yes ☐ No

If "YES," please explain. (Do not list all of the medicines that you take. List only the medicines that cause side effects.)

NAME OF MEDICINE	SIDE EFFECTS YOU HAVE
Gabapentin	Drowsiness
Tramadol	Drowsiness
Zoloft	Weight gain, constipation

SECTION E - REMARKS

Use this section for any added information you did not show in earlier parts of this form. When you are done with this section (or if you didn't have anything to add), be sure to complete the fields at the bottom of this page.

(Do not offer any additional random information)

Name of person completing this form (Please print)	Date *(MM/DD/YYYY)*
Jane Doe	00/00/0000

Address (Number and Street)	Email address (optional)
My Physical Address	My email

City	State	ZIP Code
My City	00	00000

Disability Report – Adult

DISABILITY REPORT - ADULT

PLEASE READ THIS INFORMATION BEFORE COMPLETING THIS REPORT

The office that makes the disability decision on your case will use the information you provide in this report to decide whether you are disabled. Please complete as much of the report as you can.

You may be able to apply online at: www.ssa.gov/apply.

WHAT WE MEAN BY "DISABILITY"

"Disability" under Social Security is based on your inability to work. For purposes of this claim, we want you to understand that "disability" means you are unable to work as defined by the Social Security Act. You will be considered disabled if you are unable to do any kind of work for which you are suited and if your disability is expected to last (or has lasted) for at least a year or is expected to result in death. So when we ask "when did you become unable to work," we are asking when you became disabled as defined by the Social Security Act.

IF YOU NEED HELP

You can get help from other people, such as a friend or family member. **Please do not ask your healthcare provider to complete this report.** If you cannot complete the report, you may contact us at 1-800-772-1213 (TTY 1-800-325-0778). A Social Security Representative will assist you. Have the information available from the bulleted items below when you call us. If you have an appointment, please have the information available, or the completed report ready when we contact you. If we ask you to do so, please mail the completed report to us ahead of time. **If you cannot speak or understand English, we will provide an interpreter free of charge.**

YOUR MEDICAL RECORDS

YOU DO NOT NEED TO ASK DOCTORS OR HOSPITALS FOR ANY MEDICAL RECORDS. If you have consented to us obtaining medical records from your providers, we will request your records directly from them. The information that you give us on this report tells us where to request your medical and other records.

WHAT YOU NEED TO COMPLETE THIS REPORT

- Names, addresses, and phone numbers of two people (other than your doctors) we can contact who know about your medical condition(s) and can help with your case, if needed.
- Information about any education you have completed.
- Information about all the jobs you had in the 5 years before you became unable to work.
- Any prescription or non-prescription medicines you take.
- Names, addresses, and phone numbers of any healthcare providers and information about the medical treatment you received, or testing performed.
- If you cannot remember information about your healthcare providers, the treatment you received, or the testing performed, you may be able to get that information from the telephone book, the Internet, an online medical chart, medical bills, prescriptions, or prescription medicine containers.
- If you cannot remember exact dates, provide the closest date you can remember.
- Name of organization(s) we can contact that would have medical information about your condition(s), such as Department of Veterans Affairs, social services agencies, vocational rehabilitation agencies, welfare agencies, attorneys, prisons, workers' compensation, and insurance companies who have paid you disability benefits.
- Information about any vocational rehabilitation, employment, or other support services if you are receiving Supplemental Security Income (SSI).
- **ANSWER EVERY QUESTION,** unless the report indicates otherwise: Provide as much detail as possible. If you do not know an answer, or the answer is "none" or "does not apply," please write "don't know," or "none," or "does not apply."
- Be sure to explain an answer if the question asks for an explanation, or if you want to provide additional information. If you need more space to answer any question, use **Section 11 - Remarks.**

HOW TO SUBMIT THIS REPORT

Send or bring this completed report to your local Social Security office. If you have internet access, you can locate your nearest Social Security office by ZIP code at www.socialsecurity.gov/locator. Our offices are also listed under U.S. Government agencies in your telephone directory, or you may call Social Security at 1-800-772-1213 (TTY 1-800-325-0778).

Privacy Act Statement
Collection and Use of Personal Information

Sections 205(a), 223(d), 1614(a), and 1631 of the Social Security Act, as amended, allow us to collect this information. Furnishing us this information is voluntary. However, failing to provide all or part of the information may prevent an accurate and timely decision on any claim filed.

We will use the information to determine eligibility for benefits. We may also share your information for the following purposes, called routine uses:

- To applicants, claimants, prospective applicants or claimants, other than the data subject, and their authorized representatives or representative payees to the extent necessary to pursue Social Security claims and to representative payees when the information pertains to individuals for whom they serve as representative payees, for the purpose of assisting SSA in administering its representative payment responsibilities under the Act and assisting the representative payees in performing their duties as payees, including receiving and accounting for benefits for individuals for whom they serve as payees; and

- To contractors and other Federal agencies, as necessary, for the purpose of assisting the Social Security Administration (SSA) in the efficient administration of its programs.

In addition, we may share this information in accordance with the Privacy Act and other Federal laws. For example, where authorized, we may use and disclose this information in computer matching programs, in which our records are compared with other records to establish or verify a person's eligibility for Federal benefit programs and for repayment of incorrect or delinquent debts under these programs.

A list of additional routine uses is available in our Privacy Act Systems of Records Notice (SORN) 60-0089, entitled Claims Folders System, as published in the Federal Register (FR) on April 1, 2003, at 68 FR 15784, and 60-0320, entitled Electronic Disability Claim File, as published in the FR on December 22, 2003, at 68 FR 71210. Additional information, and a full listing of all of our SORNs, is available on our website at www.ssa.gov/privacy.

Paperwork Reduction Act Statement

This information collection meets the requirements of 44 U.S.C. § 3507, as amended by section 2 of the Paperwork Reduction Act of 1995. You do not need to answer these questions unless we display a valid Office of Management and Budget control number. We estimate that it will take about 80 minutes to read the instructions, gather the facts, and answer the questions. **SEND OR BRING THE COMPLETED FORM TO THE OFFICE THAT REQUESTED IT. You can find your local Social Security office through SSA's website at www.socialsecurity.gov. Offices are also listed under U. S. Government agencies in your telephone directory or you may call Social Security at 1-800-772-1213 (TTY 1-800-325-0778).** You may send comments regarding this burden estimate or any other aspect of this collection, including suggestions for reducing the burden to: SSA, 6401 Security Blvd, Baltimore, MD 21235-6401. ***Send only comments relating to our time estimate or any other aspects of this collection to this address, not the completed form.***

AFTER COMPLETING THIS REPORT, REMOVE THIS SHEET AND KEEP IT FOR YOUR RECORDS

DISABILITY REPORT ADULT	**For SSA Use Only- Do not write in this box.** **Related SSN** **Number Holder**

Anyone who makes or causes to be made a false statement or representation of material fact for use in determining a payment under the Social Security Act, or knowingly conceals or fails to disclose an event with an intent to affect an initial or continued right to payment, commits a crime punishable under Federal law by fine, imprisonment, or both, and may be subject to administrative sanctions.

SECTION 1 - INFORMATION ABOUT YOU

When a question refers to "you" or "your," it refers to the person who is applying for disability benefits. **If you are completing this report for someone else**, provide information about them.

1.A. NAME (First, Middle Initial, Last, Suffix): Jane S Doe

1.B. SOCIAL SECURITY NUMBER: 000-00-0000

1.C. Have you used any other names on your medical or educational records? Examples include maiden name, other married names, other names, or nickname. ☒YES ☐NO

If YES, please list names used: Jane S Smith

1.D. MAILING ADDRESS (Street or PO Box) Include apartment number, if applicable.
2432 Homesteet Way

CITY	STATE/Province	ZIP/Postal Code	COUNTRY (If not USA)
MYTown	OR	12345	

1.E. EMAIL ADDRESS
myhomeemail@provider.com

1.F. DAYTIME PHONE NUMBER(S) where we can call to speak with you or leave a message, if needed. Include area code or IDD and country code if outside the USA or Canada.

Primary: (000) 000-0000 Secondary: (if available) ____

1.G. Can you speak and understand English? ☒YES ☐NO

If NO, what language do you prefer? ____

If you cannot speak and understand English, we will provide an interpreter, free of charge.

1.H. Can you read and understand English? ☒YES ☐NO

1.I. Can you write more than your name in English? ☒YES ☐NO

SECTION 2 - CONTACTS

Is there someone we can contact who can help with your claim, if needed? Examples include a family member, friend, or neighbor.

☒YES Please provide the names of two people **(other than your doctors)** we can contact who know about your medical condition(s) and can help you with your claim and can help us reach you if you become unavailable.

☐NO **We recommend that you provide at least one contact, if available.** Providing the name of someone who knows you may help us to make a decision on your claim.

2.A. NAME (First, Middle Initial, Last): John R Spouse

2.B. Relationship to the Person in **1.A.**: Spouse

2.C. MAILING ADDRESS (Street or PO Box) Include apartment number, if applicable.
Same as above

CITY	STATE/Province	ZIP/Postal Code	COUNTRY (if not USA)

2.D. DAYTIME PHONE NUMBER (as described in **1.F.** above)
(111) 111-1111

SECTION 2 - CONTACTS (continued)

2.E. Can this person speak and understand English? ☒YES ☐NO
If NO, what language is preferred?

2.F. NAME (First, Middle Initial, Last)	**2.G.** Relationship to the Person in **1.A.**

2.H. MAILING ADDRESS (Street or PO Box) Include apartment number, if applicable.

CITY	STATE/Province	ZIP/Postal Code	COUNTRY (if not USA)

2.I. DAYTIME PHONE NUMBER (as described in **1.F.** above)

2.J. Can this person speak and understand English? ☐YES ☐NO
If NO, what language is preferred?

SECTION 3 - MEDICAL INFORMATION

3.A. Separately list each physical and/or mental condition that limits your ability to work. If you have cancer, please include the type and stage.

1. Degenerative Disc Disease of lower back
2. Fibromyalgia
3. Depression
4. Anxiety
5.

If you need more space, go to Section 11

3.B. What is your height? 5 feet 9 inches OR ____ centimeters

3.C. What is your weight? 180 pounds OR ____ kilograms

SECTION 4 - WORK ACTIVITY

4.A. Are you currently working?

☐NO, I have never worked (Go to question **4.B.**)
☒NO, I have stopped working (Go to question **4.C.**)
☐YES, I am currently working (Go to question **4.F.**)

IF YOU HAVE NEVER WORKED:

4.B. When do you believe your conditions(s) became severe enough to keep you from working (even though you have never worked)? (MM/DD/YYYY) ____________ (Go to **Section 5**)

IF YOU HAVE STOPPED WORKING:

4.C. When did you stop working? (MM/DD/YYYY) 07/20/2024

Why did you stop working?

☒ Because of my condition(s).
☐ Because of other reasons.

Please explain why you stopped working. Examples include laid off, early retirement, seasonal work ended, or business closed.

Even though you stopped working for other reasons, when do you believe your conditions(s) became severe enough to keep you from working? (MM/DD/YYYY) ____________

SECTION 4 - WORK ACTIVITY (continued)

4.D. Did your condition(s) cause you or your employer to make changes in your work activity? Examples include job duties, hours, or rate of pay.

☐ NO (Go to **Section 5**)

☒ YES, When did the changes start? (MM/DD/YYYY) 05/01/2024

4.E. Since the date in **4.D.** above, have you had earnings greater than $1,550 before tax in any month? Do not count sick leave, vacation, or disability pay. (We may contact you for more information.)

☐ YES (Go to **Section 5**) ☒ NO (Go to **Section 5**)

IF YOU ARE CURRENTLY WORKING:

4.F. Has your condition(s) caused you or your employer to make changes in your work activity? Examples include job duties, hours, or rate of pay.

☐ YES When did the changes start? (MM/DD/YYYY) ______

☐ NO When did your condition(s) first start bothering you? (MM/DD/YYYY) ______

4.G. Since your condition(s) first bothered you, have you had earnings greater than $1,550 before tax in any month? Do not count sick leave, vacation, or disability pay. (We may contact you for more information.)

☐ YES ☒ NO

SECTION 5 - EDUCATION, TRAINING, AND LITERACY

5.A. Select the highest level of school completed, including homeschooling, online education, and education received in another country.

0	K	1	2	3	4	5	6	7	8	9	10	11	12	GED	College: 1	College: 2	College: 3	College: 4 or more
☐	☐	☐	☐	☐	☐	☐	☐	☐	☐	☐	☐	☐	☒	☐	☐	☐	☐	☐

Date completed: 06/1996 (MM/YYYY)

Name of school: MyHighSchool

City: Hometown State/Province: CA Country (if not USA): ______

5.B. Were you in special education? ☒ NO (Go to **5.C.**) ☐ YES (Complete below)

Dates from: ______ (MM/YYYY) to ______ (MM/YYYY)

If YES, select the last grade you were in special education.

Pre K	K	1	2	3	4	5	6	7	8	9	10	11	12
☐	☐	☐	☐	☐	☐	☐	☐	☐	☐	☐	☐	☐	☐

Reason(s) for special education: ______

The school where you were last in special education.

☐ Same as **5.A.**

☐ If different from **5.A.**, complete below.

Name of school: ______

City: ______ State/Province: ______ Country (if not USA): ______

SECTION 5 - EDUCATION, TRAINING, AND LITERACY (continued)

5.C. Have you received any type of **training** (specialized job, trade, or vocational training)?

☒NO (Go to **5.D.**) ☐YES (Complete the table below.)

NAME OF TRAINING FACILITY			PHONE NUMBER
ADDRESS			
CITY	STATE/Province	ZIP/Postal Code	COUNTRY (if not USA)
TYPE OF PROGRAM		Date Completed (or scheduled to be completed) MM/YYYY	

5.D. What written language do you use every day in most situations (at home, work, school, in community, etc.)?

English

5.E. READING - In the language you identified in **5.D.**, can you read a simple message, such as a shopping list or short and simple notes? ☒YES ☐NO

5.F. WRITING - In the language you identified in **5.D.**, can you write a simple message, such as a shopping list or short and simple notes? ☒YES ☐NO

SECTION 6 - WORK HISTORY
(If you need more space, use Section 11)

6.A. Did you have a job in the 5 years before you became unable to work because of your medical conditions?

☐NO (Go to **Section 7**) ☒YES (Complete the table below.)

List all the jobs you had in the 5 years before you became unable to work because of your medical conditions:

- List your most recent job first
- List all job titles even if they were for the same employer
- **Do not include jobs you held less than 30 calendar days**
- Include self-employment (e.g., rideshare driver, hair stylist)
- Include work in a foreign country

	Job Title (e.g., Cashier)	Type of Business (e.g., Grocery Store)	Dates Worked		Hours per Day	Days per Week	Rate of Pay	
			From: MM/YYYY	To: MM/YYYY			Amount	Frequency (per) hour, day, week, month, or year
1.	Barista	Coffee Shop	06/2022	07/2024	8	5	$19	HOUR
2.	Server	Restaurant	01/2022	06/2022	8	5	$18	Hour
3.	Products assembler	Manufacturer	01/2019	01/2022	8	5	$17	Hour
4.								
5.								

SECTION 6 - WORK HISTORY (continued)

Check the box below that applies to you.

☒ **I had more than one job.** (If you had more than one job, we may contact you for more information. **Do not** answer the questions in **Section 6.B** through **6.D**. Go to **Section 7**.)

☐ I had **only one job**. (If you had only one job, complete the questions in **6.B.** through **6.D.**)

6.B. Information about your work

6.B.1. For the job you listed in **6.A.**, describe in detail the tasks you did in a typical workday. Examples of tasks include stocking shelves, greeting customers, scheduling appointments, or maintaining records.

Took orders, greeted customers, prepared food and drinks, cleaned area, stocked shelves.

6.B.2. If any of the tasks listed above involved writing or completing reports, describe the type of report you wrote or completed and how much time you spent on it per workday or workweek.

N/A

6.B.3. If any of the tasks listed above involved supervising others, describe who or what you supervised and what supervisory duties you had. Examples of supervisory duties include evaluating employee job performance, making schedules, or maintaining time records.

I supervised 2 people. I would make schedules and maintain time records

6.B.4. List the machines, tools, and equipment you used regularly when doing this job and explain what you used them for. Examples of equipment include computer, telephone, forklift, air compressor, or meat slicer.

Coffee grinder and expresso machine.

6.B.5. Did this job require you to interact with coworkers, the general public, or anyone else? ☒ YES ☐ NO

If YES, **describe** who you interacted with, the purpose of the interaction, how you interacted, and how much time you spent doing it per workday or workweek. Examples include answering customer questions on the telephone for 3 hours per day or showing clients sale properties in person for 4 hours per day.

8 hours per day I would interact with the public and co-workers.

SECTION 6 - WORK HISTORY (continued)

6.C. Physical and environmental requirements of your work

Tell us how much time you spent doing the following physical activities in a typical workday. The total hours/minutes for standing, walking, and sitting should equal the Hours per Day reported in **6.A.** The example below shows an 8-hour workday with 2 hours standing and walking and 6 hours sitting (8 hours total).

Activity	How much of your workday? (Hours/Minutes)	Example:
Standing and walking (combined)	8	2 hours
Sitting	0	6 hours
Stooping (i.e., bending down & forward at waist)	20 minutes	15 minutes
Kneeling (i.e., bending legs to rest on knees)	5 minutes	15 minutes
Crouching (i.e., bending legs & back down & forward)	15 minutes	None
Crawling (i.e., moving on hands and knees)	0	None
Using fingers to touch, pick, or pinch (e.g., using a mouse, keyboard, turning pages, or buttoning a shirt): ☐ One Hand ☒ Both Hands	2 hours	2 hours (both hands)
Using hands to seize, hold, grasp, or turn (e.g., holding a large envelope, a small box, a hammer, or water bottle): ☐ One Hand ☒ Both Hands	6 hours	1 hour (both hands)
Reaching at or below the shoulder: ☐ One Arm ☒ Both Arms	1 hour	1 hour (both arms)
Reaching overhead (above the shoulder): ☐ One Arm ☒ Both Arms	10 minutes	None
Climbing stairs or ramps	0	None
Climbing ladders, ropes, or scaffolds	0	None

If you need more space, use **Section 11**

Tell us about lifting and carrying in this job. Explain what you lifted, how far you carried it, and how often you did it in a typical workday.

I would lift and carry gallons of milk sporadically throughout the day, boxes of coffee products once a day.

Select the **heaviest** weight lifted:

☐ Less than 1 lb. ☐ Less than 10 lbs. ☐ 10 lbs. ☒ 20 lbs.
☐ 50 lbs. ☐ 100 lbs. or more ☐ Other

Select the weight **frequently** lifted (i.e., 1/3 to 2/3 of the workday):

☐ Less than 1 lb. ☒ Less than 10 lbs. ☐ 10 lbs. ☐ 25 lbs.
☐ 50 lbs. or more ☐ Other 2/3 of work day

Did this job expose you to any of the following? Check all that apply.

☐ Outdoors ☒ Extreme heat (non-weather related) ☐ Extreme cold (non-weather related)
☐ Wetness ☐ Humidity ☐ Hazardous substances
☐ Moving mechanical parts ☐ High, exposed places ☐ Heavy vibrations
☐ Loud noise ☐ Other

If one or more boxes are checked, tell us about the exposure(s) and how often you were exposed.

Exposed to hot water and coffee

SECTION 6 - WORK HISTORY (continued)

6.D. Explain how your medical conditions would affect your ability to do this job.

With back pain, I can no longer stand more than 20 minutes at a time before I need to sit, laydown, or walk around. My fibromyalgia pain travels to different parts of my body. I have frequently flareups of swelling and pain in my hands or legs that make it difficult to sit or stand for very long; Repetitive use of my hands is limited to only a few minutes during a flare. Brain fog from fibromyalgia, I am unable to focus and lose attention frequently. When in a flare,I need extra breaks at work and often miss work for a few days.This happens at least twice per month. Depression and anxiety make it difficult to be around other people without experiencing panic attacks or disregulated moods.

SECTION 7 - MEDICINES

7. Are you currently taking any prescription or non-prescription medicine(s)?

☐ NO (Go to **Section 8**)

☒ YES (Complete the information below. You may need to look at your medicine containers.)

NAME OF MEDICINE	IF PRESCRIBED, GIVE DOCTOR NAME (IF KNOWN)	REASON FOR MEDICINE (IF KNOWN)
XYZ	Dr PCP	Pain
ABC	Dr Specialist	Inflammation
DEF	Dr Psychiatrist	Anxiety
GHI	Dr Psychologist	Depression

If you need to list more medicines, use **Section 11**.

SECTION 8 - MEDICAL TREATMENT

8.A. Have you seen or received treatment from a healthcare provider (doctor, hospital, clinic, psychiatrist, nurse practitioner, therapist, physical therapist, or other medical professional), or **do you have a future appointment scheduled**?

☐ NO (Go to **Section 9**)

☒ YES (Complete the chart(s) below)

You may find this information on medical bills, online medical chart, or the Internet.

8.A.1.

NAME OF FACILITY OR OFFICE	NAME OF HEALTHCARE PROVIDER THAT TREATED YOU
Make Me Well Clinic	Dr PCP

What medical conditions were treated or evaluated?
Back pain, fibromyalgia

PHONE NUMBER	DATE FIRST SEEN:	DATE LAST SEEN:	DATE OF NEXT APPOINTMENT: (IF KNOWN)
(001) 002-0033	01/2022 MM/YYYY	08/2024 MM/YYYY	10/2024 MM/YYYY

ADDRESS
123 Dr Corner Rd

CITY	STATE/Province	ZIP/Postal Code	COUNTRY (if not USA)
MyTOWN			

8.A.2.

NAME OF FACILITY OR OFFICE	NAME OF HEALTHCARE PROVIDER THAT TREATED YOU
MYTown Behavioral Health	Dr Psychiatrist & Dr Psychologist

What medical conditions were treated or evaluated?
Depression and Anxiety

PHONE NUMBER	DATE FIRST SEEN:	DATE LAST SEEN:	DATE OF NEXT APPOINTMENT: (IF KNOWN)
(123) 456-7890	07/2023 MM/YYYY	08/2024 MM/YYYY	09/2024 MM/YYYY

ADDRESS
543 Peaceful Dr

CITY	STATE/Province	ZIP/Postal Code	COUNTRY (if not USA)
Mytown	CA	00032	

8.A.3.

NAME OF FACILITY OR OFFICE	NAME OF HEALTHCARE PROVIDER THAT TREATED YOU
Fibromyalgia Care Center	Dr Specialist

What medical conditions were treated or evaluated?
Fibromyalgia

PHONE NUMBER	DATE FIRST SEEN:	DATE LAST SEEN:	DATE OF NEXT APPOINTMENT: (IF KNOWN)
(023) 456-9780	06/2023 MM/YYYY	08/2024 MM/YYYY	10/2024 MM/YYYY

ADDRESS
142 Hilltop

CITY	STATE/Province	ZIP/Postal Code	COUNTRY (if not USA)
Mytown	CA	00032	

SECTION 8 - MEDICAL TREATMENT (continued)

8.A.4

NAME OF FACILITY OR OFFICE	NAME OF HEALTHCARE PROVIDER THAT TREATED YOU

What medical conditions were treated or evaluated?

PHONE NUMBER	DATE FIRST SEEN:	DATE LAST SEEN:	DATE OF NEXT APPOINTMENT: (IF KNOWN)
	MM/YYYY	MM/YYYY	MM/YYYY

ADDRESS

CITY	STATE/Province	ZIP/Postal Code	COUNTRY (if not USA)

8.A.5.

NAME OF FACILITY OR OFFICE	NAME OF HEALTHCARE PROVIDER THAT TREATED YOU

What medical conditions were treated or evaluated?

PHONE NUMBER	DATE FIRST SEEN:	DATE LAST SEEN:	DATE OF NEXT APPOINTMENT: (IF KNOWN)
	MM/YYYY	MM/YYYY	MM/YYYY

ADDRESS

CITY	STATE/Province	ZIP/Postal Code	COUNTRY (if not USA)

8.A.6.

NAME OF FACILITY OR OFFICE	NAME OF HEALTHCARE PROVIDER THAT TREATED YOU

What medical conditions were treated or evaluated?

PHONE NUMBER	DATE FIRST SEEN:	DATE LAST SEEN:	DATE OF NEXT APPOINTMENT: (IF KNOWN)
	MM/YYYY	MM/YYYY	MM/YYYY

ADDRESS

CITY	STATE/Province	ZIP/Postal Code	COUNTRY (if not USA)

If you need to list more facilities or healthcare providers, use **Section 11.**

SECTION 8 - MEDICAL TREATMENT (continued)

8.B. Did any of the healthcare providers listed in **8.A.** order any medical tests for you? Include tests already performed and scheduled in the future.

☐ NO (Go to **Section 9**)

☒ YES (Select tests from the chart below)

TEST	NAME OF HEALTHCARE PROVIDER OR FACILITY	DATE OF TEST (MM/YYYY)
Blood test (not HIV)	Fibromyalgia Center	06/2024
Breathing test		
Cardiac catheterization		
EEG (brain wave test)		
EKG (heart test)		
Hearing test		
HIV test		
Speech/language test		
Treadmill (exercise test)		
Vision test		
Psychological/IQ test	Mytown Behavorial Health	07/2024
Biopsy (list body part):		
MRI/CT scan (list body part):	Make Me Well Clinic	08/2023
X-ray (list body part):		
Other - please specify:		

If you need to list more tests, use **Section 11.**

SECTION 9 - OTHER MEDICAL INFORMATION

9. Does anyone else (other than your healthcare providers) have your medical information? Examples include Department of Veterans Affairs, social service agencies, vocational rehabilitation agencies, welfare agencies, attorneys, prisons, workers' compensation, and insurance companies who have paid you disability benefits.

☒ NO (Go to **Section 10** if you are receiving Supplemental Security Income (SSI) and have been asked to complete this report; if not, go to **Section 11**.)

☐ YES (Complete the information below)

NAME OF ORGANIZATION			PHONE NUMBER
ADDRESS			
CITY	STATE/Province	ZIP/Postal Code	COUNTRY (if not USA)
NAME OF CONTACT PERSON			CLAIM NUMBER (if any)
Date of First Contact	Date of Last Contact		Date of Next Contact (if any)
Reasons for Contacts			

If you need to list other people or organizations, use **Section 11**

COMPLETE THIS SECTION ONLY IF YOU ARE ALREADY RECEIVING SSI.

SECTION 10 - SUPPORT SERVICES

Provide information about your participation in support services, if applicable. Examples of support services can include:

- An Individualized Education Program (IEP) through a school (if a student aged 18-21)
- An individual work plan with an employment network under the Ticket to Work Program
- A Plan to Achieve Self-Support (PASS)
- An individualized plan for employment with a vocational rehabilitation agency or any other organization

10.A. Have you participated or are you participating in any support services mentioned above or any other vocational rehabilitation, employment services, or other support services to help you to go to work?

☐ YES (Complete the information below) ☐ NO (Go to **Section 11**)

10.B FACILITY OR ORGANIZATION NAME			PHONE NUMBER
COUNSELOR, INSTRUCTOR, OR JOB COACH NAME			
ADDRESS (Street or PO Box) Include Suite, Building, etc.			
CITY	STATE/Province	ZIP/Postal Code	COUNTRY (if not USA)

SECTION 10 - SUPPORT SERVICES (continued)

10.C. Are you still participating in the plan or program? (Select answer below)

☐ YES Date began: ________ MM/YYYY Expected completion date: ________ MM/YYYY

☐ NO Date began: ________ MM/YYYY Date stopped: ________ MM/YYYY

Reason stopped: ________

10.D. What types of services, tests, or evaluation were provided?

Select all that apply:

☐ Vision test ☐ Psychological/IQ test ☐ Work classes ☐ Hearing test ☐ Work evaluation

☐ Other - Please explain: ________

If you need to list another plan or program, use **Section 11**

SECTION 11 - REMARKS

Please provide any additional information you did not give in earlier parts of this report. If you did not have enough space in the sections of this report to provide the requested information, please use this space to provide the additional information requested in those sections. Be sure to include the section and question number to which you are referring.

If you need additional space, use **Section 11 - Remarks (continued)**

SECTION 11 - Remarks (continued)

SECTION 12 - WHO IS COMPLETING THIS REPORT

Date Report Completed (MM/DD/YYYY)

Who is completing this report?

- [x] The person listed in **1.A.**
- [ ] The person listed in **2.A.**
- [ ] The person listed in **2.F.**
- [ ] Someone else (Complete the information below)

NAME (First, Middle Initial, Last)			Relationship to the Person in **1.A.**
MAILING ADDRESS (Street or PO Box) Include the apartment number, if applicable.			
CITY	STATE/Province	ZIP/Postal Code	COUNTRY (If not USA)

DAYTIME PHONE NUMBER where we may reach you or leave a message, if needed. Include the area code or IDD and country code if outside the USA or Canada.

CHAPTER FIVE:

WHAT YOU NEED TO KNOW ABOUT HIRING AN ATTORNEY

When To Consider Reaching Out To An Attorney

The earlier you can reach out to an attorney to handle your SSDI or SSI application process, the better. While you will certainly need an attorney to be able to obtain a favorable outcome at a hearing, many people find an attorney helpful from the early stages of application, too.

At the very least, be sure to reach out to a qualified social security attorney if your claim has been turned down, and get sound legal help with the appeal process. Social Security does allow non-attorney representatives to act in the case before the Agency. However, the non-attorney representatives are paid the same as an attorney representative, so it makes sense to hire an attorney who is trained to deal with complex issues of law and fact.

Attorney Fees

Every attorney who practices Social Security law is under the same government-regulated fee agreement. Currently, the highest fee a Social Security lawyer can charge is 25% of any back benefits that are due if your case is won. There is also a cap on how much an attorney can charge. SSA determines the cap and whether it will be raised. In 2025, the cap is $9,200.

So, an attorney can only charge 25% of back benefits up to $9,200, whichever amount is **less**, and no more, and only if you **win.** If you don't win the case, your attorney isn't paid. And if you or your attorney chooses to drop the case, the same no-fee structure applies. In some states, you may have to pay a retainer fee to cover costs such as the cost of obtaining medical records, but you should never have to pay the attorney out of pocket.

How To Choose The Right Attorney

There are benefits to both national law firms and smaller local law firms. A national law firm, such as the ones that often advertise on TV, may have more resources. They can get information sometimes easier and can potentially help facilitate the process faster, but a personal connection will likely be lacking.

For this reason, many clients find that a smaller, local law firm allows for more personal time spent with the attorney, allowing them to get a better picture of your disability, prospects, and background. The more the attorney knows about you, your disability, and your struggles, the better they can represent you before a hearing.

Regardless of the size of their firm, one major question to ask any attorney you're considering is whether or not they are able to represent clients at the Appeal Council level and ultimately in Federal Court in your jurisdiction. If so, you may be able to stick with this attorney through the entire appeals process if need be, instead of having to switch lawyers toward the end of the process.

If they don't, ask if there is an attorney they could refer you to should you appeal at a Federal level. It is difficult for claimants to find attorneys for federal court on their own. Many attorneys won't represent claimants who have been represented by a different attorney outside of their firm.

In any case, be sure you feel comfortable with your attorney, and make sure the lawyer you hire takes an active interest in your case. Working hard to get the medical care and documentation that you need and understanding each step of the process will also help your attorney do their job with greater ease.

How My Firm Approaches Client Care

The core of my professional life centers around connecting with clients as individuals. I make sure my clients can reach me through email and I make sure to get back in touch with them within around 24 hours if they have questions. I use my staff's help to process claims and access medical records, but I make the time to touch base with each client throughout their case and advise them personally.

My staff and I do our best to handle each client as though they were family members in need of help. Our compassion and love for our clients as people truly help us work together as a firm.

We understand that each person who comes to us has a unique story, a background, and situations they've faced that have brought them to this point – and our mission is to help people like you find a better quality of life by accessing the benefits they need.

CHAPTER SIX:

CLOSING THOUGHTS

One of the things that hit me hardest as a young female minority attorney was feeling that I had to live up to a certain standard. When I first started my career, much of Social Security law was practiced by White male lawyers who believed that successful female attorneys should be cutthroat and ruthless - but that's just not me.

When a judge looks at you, all cases become alike and nondescript to them. So, if you enter a hearing with a combative and argumentative attitude, you're likely to be met with resistance. Similarly, if you exaggerate symptoms and illnesses beyond the point of being credible, you're not likely to win.

Remember, *you don't need to be bedridden to get disability, and your pain level doesn't have to be at level 10 every hour of the day*. I've found that if your goal is to win, it helps to take a softer stance. Be real with your attorney, be real with the judge, be humble, be positive, and you're going to get a much better result.

It took years of practicing law to find my own rhythm in helping people with the gifts, personality, and softer side of myself that came naturally. After many years, I was finally able to see that my caring, compassionate side wasn't a weakness in the practice of Social Security law but a strength.

Once I embraced this fully, my law practice truly took off, and doors opened that I could not have foreseen or hoped for. I'm forever grateful for these experiences and for the fact that my perspective allows me to make such deep impacts on the lives of others. My hope is that all of the insight and information that I've shared within these pages will do the same for you.

INDEX

NOTES

Made in the USA
Monee, IL
03 November 2026

67387932R00085